PEOPLE VS CHESTER TYSON

PEOPLE VS. CHESTER TYSON

JOHARI ADE

SAKHU SHULE PUBLICATIONS

People vs Chester Tyson
Johari Ade

Sakhu Shule Publications
Copyright © 2017 Johari Ade

Second Edition

Sakhu Shule Publications

Catalog Information

ISBN-13   978-1-944139-07-0
ISBN-10   1-944139-07-9

2nd Edition REV 2017

ISBN-Digital 978-1-944139-05-6

Printed in the United States of America

Contents

•

Preface

When I was doing research for my first book, *Ten Generations of Bondage, Eleven Generations of Faith*, my work took me to the Shreve Memorial Library in Louisiana. As an avid genealogist, I had been there on several occasions, but on this particular occasion, my mission was to find more information about my maternal great-grandmother. I had heard many stories over the years about the grandmother that everyone called "Kitty" because of her hazel eyes, and how Grandma Kitty was a spitfire. I knew that the family had been separated in slavery, and that some of the Tyson's, Hendersons, and Petersons who lived in Grove, Louisiana, and Taylor, Arkansas were in fact brothers. My mother told me many stories over the years about living in Louisiana as a small child. She spoke many times about the fact that most of the family moved from Louisiana to Arkansas because of all of the racial strife in Louisiana. She related the story about a cousin who was supposed to be getting married on Christmas day, but was accused of killing some white people. She said that he didn't do it, and further, that the "white folks" knew who did it, but that her cousin was sent to prison anyway. I tucked all of that information away in the back of my mind, but from time to time it proved useful in my research. I was armed with that information when I was searching the newspaper archives at the Shreve Memorial Library. When I came across an article that mentioned an entire white family killed by "a bunch of negroes" in Grove, Louisiana, I started reading it because I was so horrified at the brutality of the crime. As I continued to read, I learned that the ax belonged to Mariah Tyson and that her son, Chester had been arrested. Not only had I found more information about my grandmother, I learned a lot more about our family's history in Louisiana than I had bargained for!

Johari Ade

Chapter 1

Grove, Louisiana 1916

The Louisiana sun relentlessly rained down un-yielding heat on the cotton fields below. Mariah plodded towards the fields, wiping the hot sweat from her brow with the back of her field-worn hands. She plucked the soft white bolls of fur from the stalks as she made her way towards her 21-year-old son, Chester. Reaching him, she stopped and stuffed a handful of the cotton into Chester's bulging sack. Shielding her eyes, she glanced up, towards the sky. The sun was directly over them - a sign that the noon-hour had arrived. Looking down at Chester's sack she smiled, satisfied to see that it was full. The day was young, yet Mariah was certain that the cotton that they had picked that day was well over two hundred pounds. Chester was still busily picking cotton while he hummed a cheerful tune.

"Come on now, Son" Mariah urged. "It's time to eat."

"That sounds good to me, Mama!" A hungry Chester needed little urging. He flung the burlap sack over his shoulder and headed towards the barn to add it to the work they had completed earlier that day. He loved to eat and was more than ready to take a break from the work while he got some grub. Mariah glanced over the vast field where thirty or forty hands were picking cotton. Nine of them were her own children, and most of the others were other family members. Her nephews Mark, Walter, Larkin, and Anderson were all helping out. Many of her siblings, nieces and nephews and friends all worked together on the farm. The sun was high, and intuitively, they began putting down their bags and tools, confident that it was time for a much needed meal break.

Mariah's family owned over eighty acres of land in Grove, Louisiana.

Grove was a small town about seven miles north of Minden. Mariah's sister Celia lived on the adjacent land. Celia also had eighty acres that she and her husband had homesteaded in the summer of 1909. Another sister, Georgia, lived nearby on her own eighty acres that her family had purchased in 1912. Mariah's mother Mealy, also lived nearby. She had obtained land soon after Emancipation and it had been in the family for years. Someday it would belong to her great-grandchildren.

The summer of 1916 was shaping up to be a good year. They were not rich, by any means, but they considered themselves blessed. They had plenty of food, a good home, and lots of family. They felt that they had all that they really needed. Mariah's mother Mealy had arrived in shackles on a slave ship at a very young age and always tried to impress upon her children what a blessing it was to be able to have their own land. They sustained themselves with the fruits of their own labor on the same grounds on which they once toiled during slavery. It was poetic in a way. Mariah wondered if her children knew just how lucky they were. They controlled their own life. They did not to have to wonder if someone would sell their babies away from them at any given moment.

Mariah was born in the late 1830's. She wasn't sure of the exact year, but her mother told her that she was born a few years "after the stars fell." Mariah had learned from her mother that one night during the autumn of 1833, someone was right outside their cabin justa hollerin' and cryin' raisin' such a ruckus, that everybody ran outside to see what the fuss was about. They looked up at the sky and saw what appeared to be stars falling towards the ground. Luminous balls of fire rained down from the sky above them, silently exploding just above their heads. They were certain that it was Armageddon as the fear of God struck Black and white alike. Bewildered at the sight before them, they pondered whether to run and hide or drop to their knees in prayer. Later, after realizing that their lives had been spared, they gathered their children and shared in the joy of seeing another day. From then on, they vowed to keep God in their lives because they knew He could come at any moment. For many, that night was a barometer by which to measure the various occasions in their lives. Because of the condition of slavery births and ages were rarely recorded. They would mark events and their ages with memories such as, "I was just coming into my workin' days when the stars fell." or "You were born the summer after the starts fell".

Mariah had another way to gauge her life. She was born in the south when the country was fully entrenched in slavery. She was in her late twenties by the time Emancipation came. She gauged her life as "before slavery" and "after slavery". She didn't like to think too much about slavery. It was a time that held too many bad memories. Although the work was hard, the fields weren't the worse part of it. For Mariah, the worst part was the children that were sold away from her.

She remembered picking cotton with her mother when she was about seven years old. Her mother fondly called her "Kitty".

One evening her mother didn't come back to the cabin after picking cotton in the fields. In a panic, Mariah searched all over the grounds for her Mama. Finally, another enslaved mother came and took her gently by the hand. She told Mariah that her mother had been sold away. Mariah cried until no more tears would come. She loved her mother. How could she be gone? Why didn't she say "goodbye" before she left? Who would sing to her at night when she was afraid? For that matter, who could she even turn to at those times? She felt lost. It felt as though her mother had died. She doubted that she would ever see Mama again.

Things changed for Mariah after 1865. A miracle had happened and the slaves were freed. Her mother somehow found her after freedom. It was then that her mother told her that during times of slavery she always knew that they could be separated at any moment. She had a plan in case that moment ever came. Mealy had nicknamed Mariah "Kitty," partly because of her light skin and hazel eyes, but she also knew that the nickname would stick. She also memorized a birthmark that Mariah had on her arm. The combination of those factors would be a good way to identify her after Emancipation. Her plan worked. Once Mealy was sold off, many people, especially the old folks still called Mariah "Kit" or "Kitty." Most of her nieces and nephews called her "Aunt Kit". Mealy had been able to piece things together and reunite her family.

As Mariah looked out into the fields, she was thankful that she had been reunited with most of her own children who had been separated from her during that time. Slavery was generational in the family. Like her mother Mealy, she knew what it was like to be separated from your children. Frank was her first born. She was not much older than eleven or twelve when her body betrayed her and breasts began to protrude beneath her threadbare dress. She knew that most enslaved girls bore children soon after their bodies were ripe for breeding. About a year later, Frank was born. In quick succession, she had George, Bud and Amelia, who was named after her grandmother, Mealy.

A few months after Amelia was born, Frank came up to the cabin looking confused and distressed. He said that Massa wanted the two of them to come up to the Big House. Mariah had an uneasy feeling as the two of the walked up to the house. In a flash, they found themselves shackled to a wagon and headed away from their family. Later, she heard that Frank had been sold for twelve-hundred dollars and she had been sold for eight hundred. She wondered if she would ever see her other children again.

Mariah was one of the fortunate ones, though. Most of her children were sold to neighboring plantations and they managed to find their way back to each other after freedom came.

To many outsiders, their family dynamics seemed strange. Both Mariah and her mother, Mealy had children who lived with other relatives on nearby farms. The vestiges of slavery that had allowed the breakup of the family meant that children who had been sold from their mothers often lived with the people who had raised them during slavery. Family allegiances were very fluid. Confusion often arose when Black people referred to others who had different last names as their "sons" "daughters" or "siblings". People who knew them well were often aware of the parent-child relationships. They were aware that they had different last names because they had been separated in slavery and each had kept the name of the last slave-owner, or one of their own choosing. But they were all blood kin. That was the way it was. Slavery had eradicated the ability to know whether you were related by blood or simply related by the slave-owners name.

Now, looking out into the fields, she marveled that even though Frank had been sold twice, she had found him as well as her son Bud. Frank was a Peterson, and Bud was a Henderson. And there they were, out in the fields picking cotton along with her two other sons, Leonard and Albert Tyson, who had never been enslaved and could not have imagined that life. They were having a good time laughing and joking with each other. They sauntered towards her, smiling and looking forward to the noonday meal.

"Hey Mama!" Chester had returned from the barn and interrupted her thoughts. "We sho got us a mess-a-cotton today. Good thang we did cuz I tol ol Mista Reeves' that I's going ova to his house tomorrow to make a little money cuttin' some cane fo im."

Mariah was not pleased. She didn't care for Mr. Reeves. Truth be known, she was afraid of him. Moreover, she didn't like Chester being around him. But Chester had dreams. He had his eye on a girl named Hattie who lived in Grove Town and he was thinking about marryin' up with her. Chester and Hattie had even had a child together a few years back when Hattie was only fifteen years old. But the baby died from pneumonia less than a year later. Chester hadn't been the best boyfriend at the time, but he truly loved Hattie now, and wanted to be with her. The best way to impress her was to show her that he was a hard worker who would take good care of her. Chester frequently picked up odd jobs here and there. He worked at the local mill, and even gambled a bit to pick up extra cash. However, Mariah didn't understand why Chester would want to be anywhere near Mr. Reeves, especially when just last week, he had complained that Reeves refused to pay him the money that he owed him from a card game. Besides, John Reeves was more than twice Chester's age, and white at that. Whatsoever did Chester have in common with him? Nevertheless, Chester was a man now. He could come and go as he pleased. Mariah only hoped that she had raised her son right.

"Why you gotta go ova to the Reeves?" Mariah carefully asked. They's plenty uh work round heah! "Gotta pick those greens fo' they go to seed!" she reminded him. "And I thought you had to work at the Mill tomorrow!"

"I'll get to it, Mama." Chester promised. "Jest pickin up a little extra cash, that's all."

Mariah knew that it was useless to argue. She had to let him go. At least he didn't move from town to town like Frank, her first-born son did. Frank never stayed in one place long. First, he moved to southern Louisiana and then several places in Arkansas. She was thankful that Chester stayed close to home. Sure, he drank too much at times and spent too much time at the juke joint, but she could always count on him to come home at night and help her when she needed it. She was satisfied with her life and with her children. She wouldn't complain about the little things.

Over the next few months, they got all of the fall crops harvested and they settled down for the holiday season. Christmas would soon be upon them and it would be time to begin curing the meat and baking the bread. Christmas was a special time at the Tyson house. The women cooked for a whole week. They made special gifts for each other and had a good time visiting back and forth.

A few days before Christmas, Mariah and her sister Georgia were outside gathering freshly chopped wood for the fireplace. Knowing that she was a widow, Will Hawkins, one of Mariah's neighbors had been kind enough to split the wood for her and stack it neatly just outside the door. He promised to come again soon and chop more. Mariah hoped to have a few extra cords of wood split and stacked to heat their home when the weather changed. They made extra money selling some of it during the wintertime. She noted that Will had left her ax perched and perfectly centered in the tree trunk. She would remind Chester to put the ax away when he got home so that it wouldn't rust with the next rain.

The next day was Sunday, and Christmas Eve. They would have an early church service, and then come home and continue the baking. Mariah wanted everything in order for the holidays. The wood and coal was prepped and the house was decorated for the holidays. They had been to the market and had all the flour and meal that they needed. They would tidy up a bit and she would have the boys put the tools in the tool shed for safekeeping.

Chapter 2

Christmas Eve

The afternoon sun warmed the crisp winter day as Mariah gathered fresh eggs from the chicken coop. Hearing leaves crackling down the road, she glanced up as her nephew Anderson Heard strolled towards her. Anderson and Chester were cousins and they were as close as brothers. Anderson frequently spent the night at their house, as did Chester at Anderson's house. Anderson was what the old folks called "tender-hearted." But many of the young folks weren't as kind. They called him "simple-minded." But he didn't seem to care. Most of the time, it was just good-natured teasing. Mariah liked it when Anderson came around. She loved Andy. He was a good kid. He would always offer to help do things around the house for her. But he usually did more eating and sleeping than working.

"Hi, Aint Kit!" Anderson called out to her. "Mama sent these sweet taters over for the pies. Said you's makin the tater pie fer Christmas and she said make sho you gits these."

"I bet she did!" Mariah laughed. That was just like her sister to assume that she was making the potato pie. But the pie was her specialty. Besides, she expected her sister Georgia to make the banana pudding.

"Just put em in the pantry, Andy. I'm gonna make em later."

"Yes, Ma'am." Anderson put the potatoes in the pantry and headed for the davenport to sit and rest his tired feet. "You need anything else Aint Kit?" he asked as he plopped down on the well-worn couch.

Mariah shook her head and smiled as she watched Anderson adjust the cushion and make himself comfortable while he waited for Chester to get home. She headed back to the kitchen, hoping to finish the baking so that that there would be less to do on Christmas morning. She planned to go to bed early so that she could get up at dawn the next day. She would need to get the stove fired up for the turkey. Frank had bagged them a plump 30-pound turkey that year. It was dressed and ready to roast.

Mariah cheerfully hummed as she cut, chopped, mixed and baked in the tiny aroma-filled kitchen. Hours later, she had accomplished her mission. She threw a blanket over Anderson, who had fallen asleep on the davenport, and then she headed off to bed.

Anderson was still fast asleep when Chester came in. Chester clumsily staggered into the house, tipsy from the whiskey at the juke joint. He had just left a big Christmas Eve party there. They were celebrating the holidays and Chester's impending wedding to Hattie tomorrow afternoon. He'd spent much of the night twirling around the dance floor with Hattie, and he'd had a few extra drinks to celebrate his last night as a bachelor. Tomorrow afternoon, he and Hattie would exchange wedding vows after the big holiday dinner. The party was just winding down when he finally stumbled out of the place. It was nearing eleven o'clock at night and many of the patrons had already left to get ready for Christmas day. When he walked into his house, he noticed that the front room was cold and damp.

"Hey Andy!" Chester shook Anderson's shoulder to wake him up. Anderson swatted Chester's hand away and nestled himself further beneath the blanket.

"Hey Andy!" Chester persisted. "How come you let the fire go out?" Chester was not pleased. The room was frigid and there was a stack of wood right next to the fireplace. He did not appreciate the fact that Anderson had not even tried to stoke the fire. He gave up on trying to wake up Anderson, and grabbed the poke to stir the fire. He added more wood to the fireplace and moments later warmth once again spread throughout the room. He went into the bedroom and pulled a pair of long johns out of the old dresser drawer. Returning to the living room, he pulled them on as he glanced over at the fire. His feet were still cold. He slid them into a nice pair of wool socks that were sitting by the fireplace and rubbed his hands together for warmth. He headed back towards the bedroom, hoping that he wouldn't have to push his brother Leonard off of his side of the bed. Leonard slept even heavier than Anderson did and he was always sprawled all over the bed before Chester got into it.

Chester was just about to scoot Leonard over when he heard a light tap on the front door. At first, he ignored it, thinking that it was just one of the dogs scratching to get in, and then he heard it again. He stumbled to the door and yanked it open wondering who would be coming around at this hour of the night. He found himself looking right into the eyes of his white neighbor, Henry Waller!

Henry Waller's six foot frame filled the doorway. The dingy plaid shirt that he wore smelled of stale beer and cigarette smoke. The few buttons that were left in it were sitting in all the wrong holes. His faded fedora was thin from wear and sitting at an odd angle about his head.

Henry had a silly drunken smile on his face. "Come on Chester!" he belched. "Put some clothes on. We're going over to old man Reeves place to get somethin' to drink and to play a little pitch. He's got some of that whiskey you're so fond of. We're gonna beat the pants off the old geezer and you'll be a richer man in the morning! Come on! I'll even put up the ante. Hurry up, boy! Time's a wastin."

"Mr. Henry," Chester began, "Cain't do it tonight." Tomorrow is a big day and I don't….."

"Come on now, Chester, I don't want to hear that shit!" Henry persisted. He spoke out of the side of his mouth as he tried to persuade Chester to come with him. "I need cash and so do you! And you know that Reeve's got a wad of it. And he don't mind putting it in your face either! You've seen him waving that wad around with his drunk ass. And you know he can't play worth a damn when his ass is drunk."

Henry filled his cheeks with air and hissed out a stinky burp. "And he oughta be good and drunk by now. Easy pickins! Now come on boy! He urged. Quit your bitchin' and get a move on!"

Chester was warm and cozy in his long johns. He was looking forward to snuggling beneath the covers. But he knew that Henry wouldn't take "no" for an answer. The old bastard had always expected Chester to do as he was told. That was the way things were in Grove Town, in 1916. There was a hierarchy between colored and white. Every white man was considered the boss of every black man. Chester was aware that he was expected to conform. It was rarely useful to argue.

Chester glanced towards his mother who was asleep in the next room. He wanted to get Henry away from the door so that Henry wouldn't wake her. Chester surely didn't want her to get wind of an invite to gamble at the Reeves place. He knew that she hated John Reeves. But if she hated anyone more than Reeves, it was Henry Waller. She said that there was something evil about him. She wouldn't take kindly to him standing on her doorstep in the middle of the night. Besides, Henry smelled like a brewery and Chester knew him well enough to know that when he was liquored up there was no reasoning with him.

"Allright, Mr. Henry, just a second." Chester slipped on a pair of overalls and pulled a pair of shoes over his warm socks. He grabbed the tattered jacket that used to belong to his Daddy and stepped outside the door. They headed out the back way and passed the tree stump.

"Grab that ax, will you!" Henry demanded. We might need it along the way.

Chester glanced over at Henry. He had noticed that Henry had a rifle with him. That didn't surprise Chester. You never knew what you would encounter in the woods at night.

Chester pulled the ax out of the stump. He thought that it was an odd request, but in Henry's drunken state, he didn't want to ask any questions and rile him up even more than he was. "Hurry up! Let's go!" Henry said, "We got to stop and get your cousin Mark Peters."

As the two of them walked the short distance to Mark's house, Chester was silent and glum along the way. A night with Henry Waller and Old Man Reeves wasn't the way that he wanted to spend Christmas Eve. He'd had a good time at the juke joint, and he was looking forward to a relaxing night when Henry interrupted his peace. He wondered why in the world Mark would want to spend a cold Christmas Eve playing a drunken poker game.

As they neared Mark's house, Chester saw movement in the shadows. Upon moving closer, he noticed that Mark and a scrawny white man were standing just outside the back door. He recognized the man as Johnny Long. Johnny was a few years younger than Chester. Chester thought of him as a kid. They had both done work for Waller from time to time. Johnny had lived in the Grove area for a number of years with his family.

The screen door was open and another man was coming out of the door. It was Larkin Stewart, one of Chester's cousins who lived in Grove.

"Well, well, well! I guess we got ourselves a party!" Waller's voice was jubilant, as rubbed his hands together.

"Hey, Mark," he called out in raspy voice. My feet is cold and wet. Run on back in the house and get me some more socks and some dry shoes will ya? I'll give em back to you later."

Mark hesitated a moment, looking curiously at Henry. Then wordlessly, he stepped inside the house and returned with a pair of tan shoes and two pair of socks in his hands.

"Nice!" Waller remarked, pulling on a pair of the socks and sticking the other pair into his pocket. He slipped his feet into Mark's shoes, commenting that it was good that Mark had bigger feet than his. Finished, he stood up. "Let's go!" he motioned to the others. Together, they headed down the dark dusty road. An occasional dog howling in the night and the constant sound of crickets were the only sounds heard besides the crackling brush beneath their feet.

Henry stifled any conversation as they moved along, saying that they must walk softly and silently to avoid waking the neighbors. But he needn't have bothered. He seemed to be the only one who was in the mood for talking. The others were glum as they ambled towards their destination.

Soon, they reached the Reeves home. As they inched closer, Chester had a very uneasy feeling in the pit of his stomach. The house was dim. He observed a sliver of light flickering through a huge open gap in the log frame. He assumed it was from the old kerosene lamp that was beginning to burn out.

"Looks like dey's gone to bed." he said. "Maybe we ought not bother em."

"He ain't in bed." Henry retorted. "And if he is, he'd better get up. Call him out here!"

"But Mr. Henry…." Chester started, "I don't think….."

"That's right, boy -- you don't think!" He angrily glared at Chester. Apparently, Henry decided that it was useless to argue with him. "Just hand me that ax, boy!"

Curious as to what Henry had planned, but unwilling to question him any further, Chester handed over the ax. His mind was racing a mile a minute. Why was Henry so interested in that ax? Was he going to break the door down with it or what? And why did the look in Henry's eyes make him feel like jumping out of his skin? Chester just wanted to go home. He didn't want any part of Henry Waller or John Nelson Reeves. But he was here now. And Henry was crazy. Chester hoped that the night would soon end and he could return home and just stay out of Henry's way. Damn! Why didn't he just stick to his guns and just refuse to go?

Henry glanced over at the other men and spoke in a commanding voice. "Now listen up here! I'm in control now! I'm gonna tell you all how this is gonna go down!" Henry pointed his index finger towards Johnny and then Mark. You two come with me!" Henry ordered. "And when we get in there, you do as I say and you do it fast! And you better not run or I'll blow your asses off with this here shotgun! Chester, you wait sixty seconds then go on into that room on the side where the Old Man keeps that tool chest with his money. You drag it out here and force it open!"

The sinister look in Henry's eyes and the tone of his voice startled Chester, and his heart skipped a beat. He suddenly realized that Henry's intention was certainly not to have an ordinary card game. He was gonna rob the old man!

Henry stealthily started up the steps. He peered over at Larkin and pointed to the side of the steps. "You stand over there by the side of the house. That bastard runs out – you stop him!" he ordered. Then he crooked his index finger and motioned for the others to follow him inside the house.

"Mark looked questioning at Johnny to see if Johnny had any insight into Henry's plans. Johnny had a bizarre, frightened look on his face and avoided Marks eyes. But Johnny fell in line behind Henry and then Mark cautiously followed the two of them. Henry reached the door and carefully turned the knob. It gave way and the door creaked open and they began to enter the house.

A nervous Chester stayed put. Things seemed to be quickly escalating out of control. What had they gotten themselves in to? What did Henry mean by "Do as I say?" Just what were his plans for them? Waller spun around and impatiently glared at Chester.

"You stand guard right here!" a drunken Henry said waving his finger in a circle towards the door. A confused Chester's mind was racing a mile a minute. Did Henry say, "stay here?" Didn't he just tell him to go in and get the toolbox? Hesitantly, Chester slowly started up the steps that led to the door. He turned around to see if Larkin was behind him, but a wide-eyed Larkin was glued to "his position" near the back of the porch.

The others had just entered the home when Chester reached the porch. Through the open door, the fireplace provided a gleam of light. Chester had just put one foot over the threshold when a flash of light shimmered from the ceiling in the adjoining room. Chester thought it was a stream of light from the kerosene lamp, flickering in the dark. But it wasn't the lamp. It was the ax! A glint of light from the ax had bounced off the ceiling in the glimmering light from the fireplace.

Suddenly Chester heard a lurid "Craaack!!" and then a heavy "thump" coming from the room. As he glanced across the small living room towards the bedroom, he realized that Henry had raised the ax and had brought it crashing back down towards the bed a second time. And there was someone lying on that bed! Instantly, blood spurted out from the figure laying there and flew in every direction. Simultaneously with the sound of the ax, Chester heard a baby scream. It was a frightened scream as the baby was suddenly jolted awake. The cries from the other room became louder as the infant yowled in fear. Oblivious to Chester standing in the doorway, Henry darted out of the bloody bedroom towards the sound of the crying baby.

Chester was transfixed as Henry darted towards the infant's cries. As Henry reached the door of the room, he grabbed the neck of the ax, circling it around his body and getting a firm grip on it. Once more Henry raised the ax and swiftly brought it back down towards the crib. Stunned, Chester quickly backed out of the door, stumbled across the porch, and down the steps. As he reached the bottom step, he almost knocked over a horrified Larkin who was peering through the partially open doorway to investigate the commotion. Chester's head felt like it was going to explode as multiple sounds of thuds, bumps, and screams emitted from just beyond the door of the increasingly horrifying dwelling.

Suddenly the door flew wide open and a frightened woman stood on the threshold. For a split second, she paused, apparently noticing the others standing in her yard. But in a flash she bounded down the stairs and away from the house as a crazed Henry was on her heels.

"Chester grab that chest out of the shed room!" Henry ordered as he bounded down the steps. Henry's hand tightly gripped the handle of the ax. His shotgun dangled wildly from a strap on his shoulder. In his haste, he brushed up against Larkin who quickly jumped out of the way to avoid being knocked to the ground. As Henry passed, a splatter of blood flew off the ax and onto Larkin's clothes. A horrified Larkin gasped at the scene unfolding before him. In a flash, the woman darted towards the back of the house, her feet barely touching the ground as her white nightgown billowed in the wind. Just as they disappeared around the bend, a gunshot rang out. Seconds later Chester heard a thump, and a crash, like someone falling over a tree. The next sound was a familiar one. It was the same sound that Chester had heard when the ax had come down on Reeves in the bedroom. There was a loud "whack", and then a dull thud. Then it was silent.

Moments later Henry magically reappeared in the darkness. He sauntered back towards the house, strolling along as if nothing out of the ordinary had just taken place. As Henry approached, Chester's entire body tensed as he braced for the ax that he was certain would fell him at any moment.

Suddenly remembering the others, Chester looked towards the house and saw Mark leaning against the railing on the side of the porch, clearly distressed and dazed. One hand clutched his chest as he took deep breaths, trying to gather air into his lungs as he squinted towards the frightful house. His other hand was clutching his head in disbelief.

Chester looked inquisitively at Mark, unsure if Mark had been shot or worse. Mark didn't appear to be wounded -- at least not physically. Seconds later Johnny bolted out of the house, a panic-stricken look on his face, as he surveyed the others. Mark glanced past Johnny, his eyes peering back into the house, as if trying to figure out if what he had seen was real.

Johnny had a wild, dazed look on his face. His eyes met Chester's and then he quickly looked away. He swiftly surveyed the others and then fixed his stare back to the house.

Chester couldn't move. He couldn't speak. His feet were glued heavily to the ground. Henry had reached the spot where Chester was standing. Henry had a deranged look in his eyes that was the strangest that Chester had ever seen. His eyes were red and beady and to Chester, Henry looked like the devil himself. Those eyes, the windows of Henry's soul held a psychotic, demented and just plain evil look.

"Where's the toolbox Chester?" Henry demanded.

"I, uh… I think I left it….it must be…" Chester stammered and finally just pointed in the direction of the house.

"Damn, Sissy." Henry taunted. "You're worthless!" Henry rushed back into the house and a moment later the sound of metal being dragged across the wooden floor could be heard from the open door. Within moments, there were several loud cracks that sounded like someone striking metal upon metal. Finally, Henry returned with a delighted look on his face. He was carrying a pistol.

Henry's breathing was shallow and a demonic light seemed to surround his entire body. He displayed an unnerving calmness that belied the events that had happened before their very eyes.

His usually squinted eyes had widened a bit, causing him to look even more deranged. Henry coolly ambled across the porch and walked over to a bucket filled with water that was sitting near the edge of it. He dipped his hands into the water several times and then shook them off, splattering bloody drops of water on everyone near him. Spotting a towel hanging on a nail near the porch, Henry slid it off the nail and rubbed it vigorously over his hands. After drying his hands he absentmindedly tossed the bloodstained towel to the side of the porch as the others watched, still stunned from the events unfolding before them.

"You all come here, now!" Henry demanded stepping away from the porch.

Chester felt that he was close enough to Henry already and he stayed right where he was. Mark and Johnny each took half a step closer. Larkin lagged further back.

"My God!" Henry jubilantly exclaimed as he rubbed his hands together. His chest was heaving in and out, his body clearly affected by the adrenaline that was rushing through it. However, his voice was surprisingly calm. "Boys, we played hell here tonight! Now you just keep your mouths shut and when this thing blows over in a few days I will settle up with you all. And I expect that this little 'card game' is gonna stay just between us!" he chuckled. "Cuz if it doesn't, I'm gonna kill every last one of you suckers. I swear I will if it takes me forty years to do it!" He promised. Henry reached into his pocket and retrieved the automatic pistol that he'd placed there. He lifted the pistol and waved it in Chester's direction as Chester flinched and braced for the worse.

"Here Sissy," he said, thrusting the pistol at Chester. "You take this and you hide it real good. The old man ain't got no use for it now!" he chuckled. "And you'll get rid of that ax if you know what's best for you."

Next, Henry walked over to Mark and put a hand on Mark's shoulder to steady himself. Then, using the balls of his feet, he slid off the tan shoes that he had borrowed from Mark. Reaching into his pocket he pulled out the other pair of Mark's socks, then bent down and slipped them onto his own feet.

"Hey Peters," he said flashing that bizarre, twisted smirk. "You know I always keep my word, so here are your shoes back. They're just a little discolored now." he snickered.

Finding it both peculiar and haunting that Henry could laugh off such a horrendous act with such a cavalier attitude, Mark wordlessly took the shoes, noting the dark red blood dripping slowly from the soles. Silently, he vowed to burn them at the first opportunity.

"Now I want you all to go on home, real easy-like." Henry ordered. Don't call no attention to yourselves. And you damn sure better not call no attention to me." With that, Henry motioned to Johnny and they headed off to the south. Chester, Mark, and Larkin headed off to the north, soon separating to go to their own homes. Each was left with his own thoughts to ponder the Christmas Eve that would change their lives forever.

As Chester walked home, he mulled over screams, the thuds and the horrendous sights that he had just witnessed. Convinced that he was in the midst of a dream, he prayed that the sweet smells and the joyful sounds of a beautiful Christmas day would arouse him from the horrifying visions in his mind. He had to be dreaming, he reasoned. It was Christmas Eve. Just hours ago he was at the Juke Joint dancing with Hattie and having a great time. Maybe Mama was right. Maybe he drank too much. That would explain the why this nightmare seemed so real. It was the season of joy and giving, for Heaven's sake. No one would murder an entire family on Christmas Eve, would they? Could they?

As he walked along, the smell of blood filled his nostrils and the meal that he had eaten earlier threatened to force its way back up through his belly and out of his throat. Finally, he arrived home. Thankful that all was quiet inside, he softly entered his bedroom. His brothers were sleeping peacefully, unaware of the terrible tragedy that Chester had witnessed less than an hour ago. Chester noticed the blood that was sprinkled over the tops of his shoes. Sitting down, he hastily pulled them off. He wrapped them in an old shirt and stuffed them into a paper sack. Then he felt something hard poking him in the side. Slowly, he reached into his pocket and pulled out the blood-splattered pistol. Staring at it, he tried to push the awful screams and sounds out of his mind, but violent shivers continued to move up and down his spine.

His brother Leonard had curled up against the wall on the far side of the bed. Chester was suddenly grateful that Leonard was such a sound sleeper. He did not expect him to awaken until somebody roused him up the next day. Chester quickly lifted the sheet to expose the thinly worn mattresses. He slid the pistol deep between the mattresses covering it with a lump of cotton sticking out of one of the holes. He tucked the sheet back around the bed and gave it an extra pat. An unsuspecting Leonard snorted, took a deep breath and went back to his snoring.

His mind racing a mile a minute, Chester turned and headed back towards the kitchen. He had to think. It was just a matter of time before daylight came. It was Christmas day. He remembered the kerosene lamp flickering in the Reeves home. With a sick feeling in the pit of his stomach, he realized that Ms. Reeves was probably busily baking her family's

Christmas dinner when Henry entered with the ax. Her family would arrive soon, and see a house filled with blood and gore! And what about Chester's family? They would start arriving soon as well. Chester's mother was a widow. That meant that her neighboring sons and nephews were extra careful to make sure that she had all of the help that she needed. The house would be full of relatives in just a few hours. How would he maintain a "holiday face" after all he had seen?

Deep in thought, Chester was still in the kitchen and jerked around in a panic when his cousin Anderson walked into it.

"What the hell you sneaking up on me for?!" Chester barreled. "I thought you was sleep."

"I ain't sleep. What did that white man want last night?" Anderson inquired.

"What are you talking about?" Chester was stunned. "What had Anderson heard?" he wondered.

"I heard that white man at the door. I was half-sleep but I heard you leave. Where did you go?

"Ain't gone nowhere!" Chester insisted.

"Yeah you did!" Anderson accused. "When he left, you left, too. Where'd you go?" he repeated.

"I just went outside to get some firewood -- that's all!" Chester said.

"Firewood my eye!" Anderson continued. "I waited and you didn't come back. Where'd you go?" Anderson pressed.

"Look Andy," Chester insisted. "I done tol you it weren't nothin. Now leave it alone!"

Anderson turned and went off in a huff. He flung himself back down on the davenport and snatched up the covers. Chester was glad the questions were over. Still, he was shaken. Just how much did Anderson hear? Anderson was known to follow him every now and then when

Chester was trying to ditch him. God, he hoped that Anderson had not followed him tonight.

He went back in the bedroom and lay down on his bed, but sleep was out of the question. He mulled over the events in his mind repeatedly. He could not believe what had taken place. "Never trust a cracker!" he thought. "Mama was right when she said that Henry was trouble. He prayed that she would never find out just how much trouble. He was hopeful that no one had seen them together last night as they walked through the woods. Then, even when they found the bodies, they would have no reason to suspect that Chester was involved. He didn't have no cause to kill up no white folks, and he damn sure wouldn't kill no babies. With a jolt, he thought about the crying baby. Then he thought about how abruptly the crying stopped.

Chapter 3

Dawn

At the Reeves house, seven-year-old Cody quietly climbed down off the loft. The Christmas morning light was just peeking through the clouds. "Why is it so cold?" Cody wondered. Right before bed he had gone outside and brought in some wood, just as his Mama had asked. He had stacked it neatly beside the fireplace. Mama was up late, cooking that big juicy bird. Between the fire from the stove and the fire from the fireplace, the house should still be nice and warm, shouldn't it? So why was it so cold? He figured Mama had probably gone to bed late and was still asleep. He would put a couple of logs in the fireplace and stir up a fire.

As Cody's bare toes gently touched the floor, he almost slipped on the sticky substance beneath them. "Pa musta left his plate on the floor again." he thought. He glanced over at the fireplace and a few embers of wood glowed in the center. "Good!" Cody thought. "Just a few pieces of kindling should get the fire going again!" He would get the fire crackling, then sneak into the kitchen and take a peek at the top of the old pine table and the stockings that sat in the corner. He hoped to get a glance inside of the presents that his Mama had placed there. It was his Christmas ritual. He would rise early to see what Christmas morning would bring. From the loft last night, he saw Mama stuff something inside of the stockings in the living room. Surely, one was for him. And he was determined to figure out what was in the colorful wrapped paper.

Turning towards the fireplace Cody bent down to pick up some kindling. He tossed a few pieces of it in the fire and a flame rose up out of the ashes. Just then, a soft groan came from the other side of the house. Cody walked across the small room towards the kitchen. A sticky liquid on the floor squished up between his toes. He thought the room was flooded with rain or something. Arriving in the kitchen, he could make out the silhouette of his older brother, David. He moved towards the sound just as a burst of light from the fireplace cast a mysterious glow onto the room. David was holding their baby brother Alto on his lap. They were both covered in blood! Alto's arm was sitting at an odd angle and twitching ever so slightly as he moved. He was trying to squirm out of David's arms but each time he tried, David would pull him back, cautioning him not to move. A huge gash on the top of David's head was bleeding profusely. Blood was oozing out of several huge slashes on both of his legs. More blood was dripping from his head down onto his lap. Alto's blood intermingled with David's blood and in that moment Cody could not tell whose blood was whose. David tried to sit up but he began to fall forward. Cody caught David just in time and grabbed the huge pillow that was sitting in the corner. David slumped onto the pillow and tried to speak. His voice was barely audible as he attempted to say something to Cody. "Cody…Ma..." David seemed confused

"David!? What happened!?" cried Cody. "Are you ok?" Cody tried to steady David. "David, you're bleeding something terrible!" he cried, while trying to grab a dishtowel to stop the blood from flowing.

"I…I …" David could not gather the words necessary to form a sentence. "Get Mmma... Get Ma!" he finally managed.

Cody ran into the adjoining bedroom. His little eyes were beginning to adjust to the darkness, and the fireplace had cast just enough light into the room for him to make out his surroundings. Cody could not believe his eyes. His father was sprawled face-up full length across the bed, one leg dangling down towards the floor. His skull lay split open lengthwise into two pieces, revealing a strange substance protruding from the gash in the center. Pieces of pink-tinged flesh dangled from a nearby lamp. Blood was splattered everywhere and a pool of the dark substance was starting to collect near the arch in the doorway.

A blood-curdling scream snaked its way from the pit of Cody's stomach as he took in the horrible sight. It took him a moment to realize that the terrible sound had escaped from his own lips.

"Mama! Mama!" he called out dashing from the bedroom. "Mama!!!" He ran back into the living room, slipping on the sticky liquid beneath his feet. He tripped, and stubbing his toe on the hearth, he fell down on the side of it. His other brother, five-year-old Woodrow lay slumped near the fireplace, blood forming beneath his small frame. Cody dashed back into the kitchen and David had slumped back down to the floor, trying to reach baby Alto, who had once again slid away from him. A horrified Cody dashed out of the door, crying, and screaming, hoping that someone would come and help. "Ma!?" he yelled. "Mama!!" He ran to the side of the house, hoping that his mother was out in the yard. Getting no answer and seeing no one about, he ran to the nearest farmhouse for help. The house belonged to his neighbor, Mr. J.W. Brazelton.

In a panic, sobbing and screaming, Cody ran up to the door and banged on it to get someone's attention. Mr. Brazelton yanked the door open and was stunned to find a blood-splattered Cody on his doorstep.

"Cody? What happened son?" he shrieked. "Why are you bleeding?"

"Not me," Cody said breathlessly. "Ain't my blood Mr. B." It's David's blood. David's and Alto's! They done been killed up to the house!"

"What?" J.W. could not believe his ears. Surly he must have misunderstood. But Cody repeated it.

"Pa's dead too!" he gasped. "They's all dead!"

"Please come, Mr. B.! Please!"

J.W. swiftly yanked on an old pair of trousers and slid a plaid jacket on over his pajama top.

"Charlie!" he called out to his son. "Tell, Mama that I'm going up to the Reeves, then go tell the Ward brothers to come up over there and meet me!" He grabbed his rifle, just in case the unknown was still lurking about. He ran over to Will Smith's house house and quickly filled him in on what Cody had said. Grabbing his shotgun, Will and J.W. dashed a few yards down to the adjoining farm, where he saw his neighbor, Jewell Johnson peering down the road towards him and Cody. Will was frazzled and out of breath when they reached him, but he was grateful that he might be able to enlist their help.

"What's all the fuss about?" Jewell. asked taking in the scene. "I saw little Cody uh-runnin and uh-hollerin, and yelling something about "they's dead!" What's goin on?"

"Cody's sayin that somethin' awful done happened up at his house." Will said breathlessly. "We's goin' to check it out." We might need some help though. Ya'll come on!"

The three men, with Cody in tow, quickly headed back to the Reeves place, each one terrified of what they would find there.

When they arrived, daylight was peeking out from behind the clouds. The winter sun cast an eerie shadow around the Reeves home. As they moved closer, they saw dark red splotches of blood dotting the yard, causing each man to move cautiously and carefully. Peering at the ground Jewell noticed a wet towel lying near the bottom of the steps. He bent down to get a closer look and his eyes fell upon the pink-tinged bucket of water sitting on the edge of the steps.

Alarmed at the sight, Jewell stepped up to the porch and was startled to see numerous bloody footprints leading both to and from the inside of the house. His mind flashed back to Cody's statement that his brothers,

David and Alto lay bleeding inside. Despite Cody's declarations of death, he hoped that they were still alive.

Thinking about the possibility of the hurt children, Jewell hurriedly reached for the handle of the door. His hand was just about to touch the handle when he paused with a start. His eyes gazed upon the blood-smeared doorknob, and his hand stopped mid-air, unwilling to connect with the sticky handle. He contemplated whether he should kick the door open, or call out to John Reeves. He opted for the latter.

"John? John? You in there?" he called out.

Silence greeted him in answer to the question. Shaking his head, he looked back at Will. The blood that was splattered all around the property was evidence of the horror that must have occurred inside. Jewell wasn't sure whether or not someone could be lying in wait behind the door.

Will took a step towards the door. "Jewell., I don't think you should go in there." he cautioned. "You know that the old man might be on a drunk. Looks like he mighta run a rampage or somethin' on the family. You might get shot goin in there. We best call the Sheriff to handle this."

Jewell took a deep breath and glanced back at the house. Just then, he heard a loud moan. He looked at Will, as a panic-stricken look filled his eyes. "Did you hear that?" he asked. "I gotta go in!" he stated emphatically. "If Cody's right, those kids might be bleedin' to death. I gotta go in." he repeated. He gently kicked the door with the ball of his foot. The unlocked door creaked open. He gave it another kick and it widened, illuminating the front room with a hint of the sunlight that had continued rising on the new day. He struck a match so that he could get a better look inside the house. Seeing nothing in the living room, he turned back to Will and noticed that Will's son Grady, and the Ward brothers had joined them in the yard.

"Grady," he called out from just inside the doorframe. "Why don't you take Cody back up to the house?" I don't think this is any place for a young boy.

"Will" he said, "Tell sombody to run and get the Sheriff." He struck another match and headed for the kitchen.

Jewell cautiously raised the shotgun, on alert for any sudden movements. He glanced around the house, looking for signs of anyone moving about. With the morning light glimmering from outside, Jewell could see an overturned chair and beer cans strewn about the floor. As his eyes adjusted to the darkness, he heard whimpering sounds coming from near the kitchen and he rushed towards the sound. In disbelief, he looked down and saw David propped up against the wall with an infant halfway on his lap. A bloody David was barely conscious, but breathing. His baby brother Alto softly whimpered as blood oozed out all over his little body. Jewell moved in closer and knelt over the boys, horrified at the sight of all the blood. He hoped that the slight up and down movement of David's chest was a sign that he would be ok. He was encouraged that the baby had whimpered. Jewell noticed that Alto's tiny fingers were bloody, but moving. He was hopeful for both of them.

"Hang on boy's!" he shouted. "We're gonna get some help!"

Jewell rushed back outside to the porch, this time oblivious to the blood stained door.

"Get Doc Tomkins!" he yelled in the direction of the crowd who was beginning to gather. These boys are badly hurt. "Did somebody go get the Sheriff?" he shouted to no one in particular. "Will! Get in here and help me!" he cried.

The neighbors were starting to come from all directions, some on foot, and some riding up on their horses. Between Cody's screams and the small town grapevine, word had spread quickly. Will turned to a man on one of the horses, yelling at him to go make sure the doctor was coming. The man quickly rode off, and Jewell ran back into the house.

Jewell had checked the rest of the small house and had just reached the doorway of the bedroom, when Will entered the living room. Jewell glanced at the bed, mortified at what he saw. His hands flew over his mouth to stifle the involuntary shriek that was trying to force its way beyond his throat. His eyes widened as he stared into the bedroom in bewilderment. He couldn't believe what he saw. He felt sick in the pit of his stomach at the sight in front of him. John Reeves was sprawled across the bed, his skull cracked in two. His body was hacked all over, and pieces of flesh dangled from his body, and about the floor.

Hearing the wails that Jewell thought were inaudible, a stunned Will rushed to the bedroom door and looked past Jewell. Shocked, he violently shook his head in disbelief and pressed both hands into his belly, in an attempt to push back the regurgitation that was forming in the bottom of his gut. Taking big, deep breaths, he rushed out of the bedroom so that he could get a gulp of the outside air before he collapsed from the unbearable sight.

In his haste, he stumbled over a crumpled rug that was lying near the hearth of the fireplace. One knee hit the floor as he braced himself from falling. As he attempted to get up, he noticed another body; a child who looked to be about 5 years old. Astonished, he called over to Jewell.

"Jewell!" he cried. "Come look here. I think it's Woodrow." Jewell took a few quick steps and bent down over the boy. The boy was loosely wrapped in a blanket and the blanket was wet and bloody. Jewell placed two fingers on the boy's neck. He couldn't locate a pulse. And the boy wasn't moving.

"Oh my God! My God!" Jewell cried. It was too much. Never had he seen such a gruesome sight! He tried to force down the big lump that had formed in his throat.

He rushed outside with Will close behind him. "Where is that doctor?" he shouted.

He rushed back into the house and into the kitchen. He plucked Alto from David's lap and placed him into Will's outstretched arms. Then he picked up David. "We've got to get these kids some help!" he cried. He and Will carried the boys outside and carefully down the steps of the porch.

"It's bad!" he stated to no one in particular. "Whoever done this is gone, but we gotta get these boys some help."

The widow Foster stepped forward. "Take em up to Mrs. Browdard's house. She can help em whilst we are waiting on the Doctor."

Jewell and Will headed down the road to take the boys to the Browdard's house. Once they got there, the women got a pail of water and clean towels to bathe the wounds. They fashioned tourniquets to try to stop the blood. Jewell and Will headed back to the house.

Coming down the road towards them, Jewell spotted a dark automobile, bumping along the rugged dirt road. He felt a sense of relief as he recognized the vehicle as the one belonging to Doc Tompkins.

He quickly briefed the doctor on what he had found and pointed him in the direction of the Browdard's house. Then he rushed back into the house to retrieve Woodrow. Jewell emerged with the boy and directed one of the other men to take him up to the Browdards so that Doc could get them to the hospital.

Jewell looked up and was grateful to see that A.H. Phillips, the county sheriff, had arrived. He was questioning Will, who was breathlessly filling him in on what they had found inside of the house. Phillips motioned for Jewell to join them.

"The coroner is on his way." He was saying. "According to Smith, John Reeves is dead, and there is no sign of Mrs. Reeves. I want you to round up a posse and check this entire area. If you see anything or anyone out of the ordinary, I want you to let me know right away."

Sheriff Phillips was doing his best to establish order to the gathering crowd as he began his mission to locate the person or persons who had committed this heinous act. As Doc spirited the children away to the hospital, he turned his attention back to the crime scene. Knowing that there was nothing that could be done to save John Reeves, he hoped that Ms. Reeves had escaped and could tell them what had happened. Finding her was their next order of business.

He had barely begun surveying the damage in the house when he heard a shout outside near the barn on the other side of the property. Bolting around the back, he found several of the men huddled around a woman who was lying face down on the ground. He squeezed through the crowd and saw the woman. He instantly recognized her as Maude Reeves, the 30-year-old wife of John Nelson Reeves. Dark red blood covered the white nightgown that was sticking to her body. Near her right temple, a bullet hole gaped open and more of the red substance oozed from the wound. Sheriff Phillips took a deep breath and kneeled beside her, trying frantically to locate a pulse. However, she had no pulse. Her lifeless body eradicated the hope that she had escaped and would be able to tell them what had happened on that terrible night. Sheriff Phillips felt helpless and completely devastated!

Never had he processed such a horrendous crime scene. Everyone was looking to him for answers. Silently, he vowed that someone would pay for this unspeakable crime.

Observing the growing crowd gathered around him, Sheriff Phillips went into action. Enlisting their help might provide some clues. At the very least, it would distract their attention away from him and the gruesome part of the crime scene.

"I want you all to get into groups of three or four." He began. "Then I want you to fan out and look carefully for anything that appears out of order. It appears that Mrs. Reeves has been shot and hacked with some kind of ax. I want you to look for any kind of gun, ax, machete, or any type of weapon that might have been used."

Looking around, Sheriff Phillips noted the bloody footprints leading away from the house. He tried to count the footprints. There were clearly at least three sets. He noted that one set was somewhat smaller than the rest, and probably belonged to a child. Mrs. Reeves was barefoot, so he knew that the prints were not hers.

Bright red discolorations of blood were scattered about the property, and huge blotches of it sprinkled the porch and the surrounding grounds. Several of the bright red footprints pointed south, but they stopped abruptly near the property. Other footprints formed a trail headed in the opposite direction. He was confident that the footprints would lead him directly to the door of the monster or monsters who had committed this heinous crime.

CHAPTER 4

SUNRISE

Chester lay on the bed, but had not slept a wink when the sun began to fill the room. It was dawn. It was Christmas day. And he was terrified at what the day would bring. He stepped into the kitchen just as Mariah was placing the huge turkey into the oven. After settling it on the rack, she stuck her palm inside of the big pot-bellied stove and a frown fell across her face.

"Stove's not hot enough." she stated. "Chester, will you run outside and bring in some more wood?"

"Yes, Ma'am" Chester complied. He stepped outside and around back. He immediately noticed the empty tree stump where just yesterday the shiny ax was perched safely in the middle. His mind flashed back to the glint of that ax coming down over Mr. Reeve's body. He pushed away the thought and gathered the wood. He turned and made his way back towards the house with it.

Off in the distance he noticed a steady trail of the neighbors headed in the direction of the Reeves house. Some were on horseback and some were on foot. Startled, he dropped the wood and stretched his neck to get a better look. Mariah came to the door.

"What's taking you so long, Chester?" she scolded. "This bird ain't got all day to cook. Hurry up with that wood, son!"

Chester picked up the wood and quickly went inside. He put it in the kitchen and then headed to the porch to wake a sleeping Anderson.

"Andy! Hey Andy! Wake up!" he shouted as he shook his cousin. Anderson grunted and turned his back to Chester. "Leave me alone!" he mumbled. "Let me sleep!"

Chester was not deterred.

"Andy!" he shook him again. "You gotta wake up! Come on now!" He shook him harder and finally Anderson angrily sat up.

"Why!!??" he demanded. "It's Christmas! We ain't gotta work today!"

"I got something important I need you to do." Chester breathlessly begged. "And I'll pay you! I'll give you 50 cents if you get up right now and do me a favor."

Anderson rubbed his eyes and yawned. He could use a little Christmas money. Besides, he was fully awake now. At least he could hear Chester out.

"What do you want me to do?" he asked.

"Something is going on up the road." Chester explained. "I want you to go and see what all the fuss is about."

"What fuss?" Anderson inquired.

"If I knew what was going on, I wouldn't need you to go figure it out!" Chester said impatiently.

"Why can't you go?" Anderson countered. "I needs my rest. And fifty cents ain't gonna get me nothing I need! I'll go for two dollars." he countered.

"Ok!" Chester quickly agreed. "I'll give you a dollar now and a dollar later."

Anderson sat up straight. "Let me see the cash!" he demanded. He didn't trust Chester to follow through on the promise.

Chester ran to his coat pocket and pulled out a rumpled dollar bill. "Here!" he said. "Now hurry up and go!"

Anderson yawned and pulled a pair of overalls over his long johns. Two dollars sounded okay for 15 minutes work. Just to walk up the road and see what the neighbors were up to? He could do that, come back, and get some more sleep. Then he could hold the other dollar over Chester's head when he needed to.

Chester impatiently pulled Anderson to his feet and pushed him out of the door. He watched him until he was out of sight. He was frightened that the sheriff would soon be questioning the entire neighborhood. He had to know what, if anything had been discovered at the Reeves. Then he remembered the pistol that he'd hidden between the mattresses. Quickly he ran into the bedroom, thankful that Leonard was still sound asleep. He pulled out the pistol and grabbed a towel. He quickly wiped the pistol clean and slid it back in its hiding place.

After what seemed like forever, Anderson returned with a wild, confused look on his face.

"A whole bunch of white folks and da law is over to the Reeves." He reported. "They's sayin' somebidy done killed up the whole family. They say that old man Reeves been hacked to death! They done called the Sheriff and da coroner!" he breathlessly reported.

"Damn!" Chester's head felt like it was going to explode as sheer panic overcame his body. He began to pace the floor.

"I know they's gonna blame me for it." he mumbled to himself as he kicked the door shut. But Anderson heard his rantings.

"What you mean 'blame you'?" he inquired. "What you know about killin some white folks?"

"Don't know nothing!" Chester insisted. "But I work for Reeves and everybody knows that Reeves plays cards with colored folks ever now an then. You know they'll blame a nigger for anything that goes wrong in this town. We best be ready, that's all."

Anderson looked curiously at Chester. He knew something was up. He might be slow but he knew when something wasn't right. And Chester was acting stranger than he'd ever seen him. Chester was usually cool as a cucumber and calm as they come. Now he looked like he was going to jump out of his skin any minute.

"You went to play cards with Old Man Reeves last night, didn't you?" he accused. "Admit it. You seen who done it."

"I told you, Andy!" Chester reiterated. "I ain't seen nothing, and I don't know nothin. Why don't you just forget the whole damn thing?"

A knock on the door interrupted their conversation. It was Chester's brother Bud, coming to put the tables together for the family Christmas dinner. Anderson opened the door for him.

"Sho is a lotta ruckus up at the Reeves place this morning." Bud remarked. "They is saying Miss Maudie was found dead in her back yard. I wonder what happened?"

"Ask Chester." Anderson suggested. "He been over to the Reeves las' night."

Chester glared at Anderson. He should have known better than to have Anderson go check things out. But he was desperate. The last thing he needed though, was his older brother asking questions. However, it was too late.

"You know something about it, Chester?" Bud questioned. "Cuz if you do, you know how talk goes around this town. What you know about it?"

"Nothing!" Chester insisted. "I keep telling ya'll I DON'T KNOW NOTHIN!"

However, Bud knew his brother well enough to know when he was lying. Chester was about to jump out of his skin and was on the verge of tears. And he kept glancing towards the kitchen, hoping that Mama wouldn't come in and hear their conversation.

"Look." Chester finally conceded glancing at Anderson. "Waller did come by last night and he wanted me to go to the Reeves house to play some poker. He said Reeves had a lot of money and we could win it off 'im. But I came home when I seed the lights was off. I don't know nothing else!" he insisted.

Bud was shaken by this news. He thought that Chester knew more about it then he was saying. Bud had once seen one of his cousins pulled from his home and taken to the woods by a mob of whites. The cousin had been accused of beating a white man, and was never heard from again. Bud was a lot older than Chester. He had seen a lot over the years. And none of it was good.

"Look Ches." He began. "You know damn well the first thing they gonna do is question every nigga in this town. Any hint that you was even near the place is enough to get you strung up. This is bad -- real bad. Now if they show up you don't tell 'em nothin', you hear? Don't say a mumblin' word about being nowhere near that place 'til we figure this thing out. I'm gonna run up to Taylor and get Frank. You lay low until we know what's goin on. I'm sure they gonna put you in it some kinda way."

Bud got on his horse and rode as fast as he could to the nearby Harris farm. He knew that Green Harris had a Model T automobile that could get him to Taylor much faster than his horse could. Green didn't use it much, other than on Sunday, or an occasional trip to town. He readily agreed to let Bud borrow it. Bud quickly cranked up the automobile. With the tires bumping heavily on the dirt road and kicking up dust, he headed north to nearby Taylor Town. He had to get to their older brother Frank. Frank would know what to do.

Frank was sound asleep when Bud arrived. He awoke to Bud's loud pounding on the front door. "Frank! Frank! Open the door! Hurry up! Open the damn door!" Bud shouted.

An agitated Frank recognized Bud's voice and leaped out of the bed.

"What the hell is wrong with you, Bud?" he demanded. "You trying to wake the dead?"

"Frank! You gotta come back to Mama's with me. Chester's in big trouble and I know they gonna try ta lynch 'im." Bud cried as he rushed through the door. "They's gonna say Chester killed all those white people and they gonna be looking to skin his hide!"

Frank was wide awake now! He knew that any allegation of wrongdoing against whites could lead to a lynching. He grabbed his pants, yanking them on over his pajamas.

"Killed what white people?" he shouted as he adjusted the waistband.

Bud quickly filled him in about Chester and the Reeves.

"Ches says he don't know nothing about it but he admits he was ova there last night." he recounted. "The whole town is up at the Reeves house right now! They's sayin' that Old Man Reeves and Miss Maudie been hacked to death." he took a deep breath. "They sayin' that all the chillins is on da way to the hospital." He finished, visibly shaken by enormity of the situation.

"My God!" Frank was astounded as he listened to Bud.

"The law and them dogs will be on the hunt!" Bud continued. "It's just a matter of time before they pick up Chester's scent. Lawd knows what they gonna do to 'im."

Frank grabbed his gun and slid it into his waistband. He didn't know what to expect when he arrived in Minden, and he wanted to be ready to protect himself and his family.

The two of them ran out of the house and hopped into the automobile. Both were very worried about their brother. As they rode along, they pondered Chester's fate. Not only was Chester's future questionable, they knew that any of them could be jailed, even just for suspicion. And once they were jailed, they had a bigger problem. There was no guarantee that the lynch mob could be kept at bay.

The forty-minute drive from Taylor to Grove seemed like an eternity. Frank and Bud rushed into the house and found their mother in tears, staring at the uniformed men in Chester's bedroom.

"They's here about Chester!" she wailed. "They think he had somethin' to do with some killins'!"

The sheriff and several deputies were tearing apart Chester's room. They were searching through drawers and underneath the bed. After a few moments, Deputy Robert Carstar lifted the top mattress. He pointed his flashlight between the mattresses , and swiftly called out to the sheriff.

"Hey, Phillips!" he shouted. "You'd better come take a look at this."

Sheriff Phillips walked over to the bed and bent down, peering into the opening while Earl Taylor shined the flashlight. He stuck his hand inside. He glanced up at Chester and shook his head.

"Come here boy!" he demanded. Chester walked slowly towards the bedroom and stopped dead in his tracks at what he saw. The gun was in full view and the mattress had been ripped open.

"This here your pistol, boy?" the sheriff gruffly asked.

"Well, it's uh…it's uh..." Chester struggled to find the words.

"Never mind!" the sheriff bellowed. "You can tell us about it down at the jailhouse!"

The deputy bagged the gun and Sheriff Phillips turned to question Chester. Now, do you want to tell me where you were last night and early this morning?" he asked. "We ain't saying you done nothin, but we jest want you to tell us what you know."

"I told you." Chester replied. "I don't know nothing about no killins!"

"Oh yeah?" the sheriff answered sarcastically. "Let's go down to the jailhouse and talk about it." He nodded to the deputy who cuffed Chester and led him towards the door.

Mariah began to weep. She was horrified and she was confused. Several of her son's had had brushes with the law before, but nothing like this. She glanced at Frank and Bud, her eyes pleading with them to talk some sense into the sheriff. They looked at each other, helpless to intervene.

Both Frank and Bud recognized the sheriff. Both had been arrested by him before. Frank was arrested for retailing liquor without a license. It was true that Frank made his own wine with the fruit from their orchard. And he drank plenty of it. But retailing it? Not a chance! Everybody in town made their own liquor. Frank felt that his real crime was spending time visiting his family in Louisiana. Frank had moved just across the State line to Taylor, Arkansas years ago because of a law that said that "negroes could not own or rent their own land" in their Shreveport town. If white folks didn't like you, or thought you were trouble, they enforced the law. The Sheriff had run him out of town personally. The laws had changed since then, and many of his relatives had even received land patents from the government, but many of the whites in the community were still mad as hell about it. The sheriff hated Frank. Frank knew that nothing he could say could get Chester out of this mess.

Now the sheriff was glaring at both him and Bud.

"Frank?" asked the sheriff. Where were *you* last night?

"I was in Arkansas, preaching a sermon at the *Church* in front of the *whole* congregation." he answered, emphasizing every word.

Frank knew where this line of questioning was going. Bud had told him that police would be questioning every Negro in town, and he wasn't surprised that he was suspect.

The sheriff removed his handcuffs from his belt. Frank stepped back, distressed to find himself facing the prospect of spending a night in jail. Although he had a church full of witnesses, he knew it didn't matter. At least not yet. Not when white folks were dead and colored folks were handy. He braced himself for the handcuffs.

"Anderson Bud Henderson," the sheriff stated moving right past Frank and heading for Bud. "You are being detained for suspicion in the murders Mr. and Mrs. John Henry Reeves. Now would you like to tell us why you were near the Reeves house this morning?"

"No Sheriff!" Mariah cried pleading with the law. "They ain't had nothin' to do wit dat! Don't take my boys! Please don't take my boys."

"Ma'am, your boys got some explainin' to do!" the sheriff answered.

"Let's go!" he cuffed Bud and pushed him out of the door. They stumbled down the steps as Bud struggled to turn and talk to his mother.

"Don't worry, Mama," he shouted as he was led away. "I ain't done nothin! I'll be back! Don't worry! I'll be back!"

Mariah wept as the sheriff led her sons away. Two of her sons were now suspects in the murder of a white family. A crowd was beginning to gather outside. Many of the neighbors had seen the sheriff's automobile and had come over to check and see if things were ok. With the community grapevine at work in Grove, it was just a matter of time before the whole town was talking.

Mariah hastily threw the latch on the door, afraid that someone would come bursting through it. She slumped down onto the couch, sobbing. She feared that she would never see Bud or Chester again. She was certain that they would either be hung by the law or killed by the lynch mob. Frank tried to comfort his mother.

"They cain't hold 'em Mama." Frank cried. You know they ain't done nothin. They'll be back soon, Mama. You'll see."

"They ain't neva comin back!" she asserted. "I seen dat look in Chester's eyes. He know'd dis was comin'. I tol' him that hanging around with them white folks was trouble but he jest wouldn't listen. And he was acting real strange this mornin'. I kept asking him what was wrong.

He kepta saying 'Nothing' but I know'd something was bothering him."

"I know, Mama," Frank said. "I been tellin' him not to put his trust in any of them white folks! Something goes wrong and they use you as a scapegoat jest cuz they can. I told Chester not to be goin round there!"

"That boy don't listen!" Mariah agreed. "But I know'd something was wrong dis moanin'! I heard a big ruckus going on up the road. I got up and walked over yonder to see what all the fuss was about."

"Did Chester say anything about it?" Frank inquired.

"Not a word!" Mariah said. "I asked him if he heard all the noise. He said he didn't, and then I looked up the road and saw some men in a wagon headed towards Minden. There was a young'un wit em but I couldn't tell who it was. But I heard Chester talkin' to Andy about some trouble he might be in. He said he didn't do nothing but that he might be in some trouble with the law. I thought something had happen up to that juke joint!" she said emphatically. Now da law done taken him for murderin dem white people!? Lord, have mercy! They gonna kill im! I know they gonna kill im!" she cried.

Just then, they heard a knock on the door.

" Kitty? Kitty?? Open the door! " Mariah recognized her sister Georgia's voice." She rushed to the door and pulled the hook out of the latch.

"Kit, they got im!" cried Georgia. "The law done arrested our boys Mark and Arlicious. And Walter, too! What them boys done got themselves into?" You know that half the time they go up to that jail, they don't neva come back no mo!" she cried. "Where is my son? Is Andy here?"

"Andy is fine. He's here." Mariah replied. "But they just took Chester and Bud. You say that they took Arly, too?" Mariah was flabbergasted. Arlicious was Bud's son. He was Mariah's fourth grandson. Bud was gonna be beside himself when he heard that his son was in jail, too! Arly had just turned 21. Now he was accused of murder? "I'm gonna get to the bottom of it, Aunt Georgia," promised Frank. "Like I told Mama, dey cain't hold em if dey ain't done nothin!"

"Don't kid yo'self, boy!" Georgia cautioned. "Dey can always kill em first and ask questions later. You be careful, too! Black men ain't safe round here now!"

"I'll be careful, Aunt Georgia," Frank promised as he bounded out the door and down the steps. Although he wanted to go up to the Reeves house to see what was going on, he knew that it was the last place he should be seen. He was sure that the place was surrounded by cops and press. Any black man near the area was subject to be arrested, or worse.

His first stop was Hattie's house. There would be no wedding today. Hattie crumbled into a heap when Frank told her that Chester had been arrested for murder. Frank tried to assure her that the arrest was probably temporary but he saw the fear in her eyes. Unbeknownst to Frank, Hattie was pregnant!

Next, he went back to Taylor to spread the word about what had transpired so far. Many people in Taylor had relatives in Minden and Grove. They would want to know. He went to several houses to fill them in on what had happened. He was sure that they would pass the word to everyone. That done, he headed back to Grove.

It was nearing dusk when he arrived. He headed straight for the Juke Joint. It was the go-to place for community gossip. He knew that it would be jam-packed with folks now. They would be talking about the murders. He was right.

He stuck his head in the door and looked around. The music was playing soft and low, not blaring like it usually was. People were huddled in groups, some crying, others clearly agitated. There was one thing that was clearly out of place though. White men in uniforms were in the midst! And not just any white folks. It was the law! They were questioning some of the patrons, while others hung back, trying to hear what was being said. Frank decided not to approach, choosing instead to hang out unnoticed in the corner until they left.

Finally, they made their way out of the door, and Frank came out from behind the shadows.

"What did them crackers want?" Frank slid into a seat at the bar and directed his question to the bartender.

"They's questioning everybody about some murder!" he said.

One of the men at the bar leaned behind the other one and spoke to Frank. There was fear in his eyes and he was shaking his head in disbelief.

"They is sayin that a buncha negroes done axed up the Reeves family. Sayin that some of em been took to jail but they don't know if they can keep em safe, cuz the niggas is blamin some white men. They's a mob around the jailhouse! Sayin dat dey know who done it cuz dey got proof! They's threatenin' to take us all to jail lessen we tell em who done it cuz dey figure it had ta been a 'whole bunch niggers!" he finished breathlessly.

"They gonna lynch us all, man," cried Leonard from the booth near the bar. "They gonna lynch us all!"

"Ain't nobody gonna get lynched!" Frank stated emphatically, but not quite convinced himself.

"They's gonna figure this thing out, and find out that we didn't have nothin' to do with it. My brother Chester and everyone else will be home just as soon as it's cleared up. We's gonna be fine!" he insisted, trying to believe his own hype. "Chester left this joint and went straight home last night. Why would he go from dancing and having a good time with his girl, to axing up some white folks? That don't make no sense."

"Bring me a beer!" He yelled to the waitress, as he walked across the room and slid into the chair across from Leonard.

The atmosphere at the Juke Joint was anything but jovial that evening. Everyone clustered in groups trying to piece together the events that had transpired. They were frightened by the possibility that the Klan would rise up and burn down their homes, taking justice into their own hands. They were fully aware that very often, the Klan and the law were one and the same. And they knew that the trouble had just begun.

Frank and Leonard left the Juke Joint and headed back to Mariah's house. Yesterday, they had been making made plans to have a family get-together there and have a good time. But there was no joy in the house today. Today, there would be no Christmas celebration.

It was quiet when they arrived. They stepped into the front room and found Frank's mother Mariah and her sister Georgia sitting on the couch and wringing their hands. The meal that Mariah had prepared was still in the kitchen. Mariah had served an occasional slice of pie or a turkey sandwich to friends or relatives who stopped by to console them. The table, which earlier had been set for a big Christmas dinner had been stripped bare of decorations.

When Frank and Leonard walked in, Mariah and Georgia sprang to their feet hoping that there was news from the Juke Joint about Chester and Mark. Mariah looked at Frank, her eyes pleading for him to tell her that it had all been a mistake. Frank shook his head.

"Sorry, Mama." he said. "Nothin but bad news." He sat down in a chair next to the table and told her what he'd heard at the Joint.

"Dey is sayin that one uh dem boy's they arrested is blamin some white folks for doin the killin." Frank said sadly. He was surprised by the news and trying his hardest to wrap his head around it.

"I don't know which is worse for em -- being accused of murder or accusing a white man of murder." he glanced at his mother and thought that he'd better interject something positive into the conversation

"But, I really don't think that this time it will be about race." He continued. The law is gonna want to find whoever done this, white or black. It ain't gonna be about race." he repeated.

"It WILL be about race!" Mariah stated emphatically. "It's ALWAYS about race. And the minute word gets out that them boys is raisin' the slightest hint that white folks done it, they gonna string 'em up -- then they's comin afta the rest of us!" she put her hands over her face, and shook her head, distressed by this bit of news. "Done seen it. Done seen it all my life!" she sobbed.

"But not this time, Mama!" Frank insisted. "A whole white family done been hacked to death. Got little kids layin' up there at the hospital. Might all be dead from what I heard. It ain't gonna be about race!" He reiterated.

Even though Frank hoped that his words would comfort his mother, he had his doubts. Race had always been a factor in his life. One of his earliest memories was when he was eight years old. It was during slave times. He was riding on the back of a wagon with his uncle as they crossed paths with two white men and a boy about Frank's age. The white men were riding horses and carrying rifles. Frank remembered the little boy smiling an excited grin. He raised the rifle and pointed it at Frank.

"Is it my turn, Daddy?" he asked. "You said that it would be my turn to shoot the next coon."

Startled, Frank had closed his eyes and braced for the worse. However, the trio laughed and rode off without firing a shot. At the time, Frank was just a small boy who was enslaved on the Newsome plantation. Nevertheless, he remembered how powerless he felt that day. Not much happened when whites wanted to "shoot coon."

In his eyes, the power structure had not changed all that much in the south. He glanced over at Anderson who had a strange look on his face. Anderson was thinking about his own past as a small boy. He hadn't experienced the same things that Frank had, but he had seen a lot as a Black male in the south. He whole-heartedly agreed with Mariah. He too, had been there when his cousin was lynched and he was afraid now, that the scene would be repeated.

"Ain't nothin worse than pointin' a finger at a white man." He looked Frank straight in the eye. "You remember what happened to Riley, don't you?" he asked, remembering the incident.

Frank did remember. Riley had been accused of murder. He said that a white man did it. There was eyewitness and material evidence as proof that a white man had committed the crime. Nevertheless, Riley had been taken to jail and never heard from again. The white man who he had accused still lived happily in the neighborhood, providing living and breathing proof of the way things were.

Mariah sat back down and held her head in her hands. Like the others, her mind had scanned past events in the community. Her thoughts flashed to the horror of black men swinging from ropes on trees.

Johari Ade

CHAPTER 5

SUSPICION

L ord, have mercy." She cried. "We don't need no mo hangins!"
It was a sleepless night in the Tyson household. They talked well into the night, finally retiring about 3 o'clock in the morning.

At dawn, Mariah arose to start breakfast for her family. No one had much of an appetite for food, so Mariah just kept a pot of hot water going for tea and Postum. They returned to the discussion that they had been having last night, and wondered how the men had fared in jail overnight. They were still debating the possibility of white men involved in the killings when they heard a knock on the door. Believing it to be more friends or relatives, Mariah unlatched the door and pulled it open. Startled, she looked down to find the sheriff staring back up at her. Standing behind him was Will Hawkins, one the neighbors who cut wood for her on occasion. He had a distressed look on his face, but Mariah wasn't sure if it was fear or shame. He looked down at the ground.

"Mrs. Tyson, do you have an ax that you use to cut your wood?" the sheriff asked.

"Yes, Sir. I do." she answered haltingly.

"May I see that ax, Ma'am?" Sheriff Phillips looked past her, noticing that Anderson and Frank were standing behind her.

"Yes, Sir." Mariah stepped off the porch and led them around back to the tree stump. She had seen the ax there just a few days ago when she asked Chester to put it away. She looked down at the tree stump. There was a long slit in the center of it where the ax had been. But there was no ax. Mariah walked over to the side of the tree stump and peered at the ground. The ax wasn't there!

"Maybe it's in the shed where…" She began. "She darted over to the shed and pulled it open. The ax was not it its designated spot. "Well, let me look over by the old oak tree. Sometimes they….." her voice trailed off as she headed in the other direction.

"No Ma'am," Sheriff Phillips said, stopping her. "We believe that your ax was the one used in the murders of the Reeves family. Can you come with me to identify it please?"

Stunned, Mariah reached for the tree stump to steady her shaking body. "Where was that ax?" she thought, refusing to believe the sheriff.

Frank and Anderson had followed them outside and were standing behind her. They had witnessed only part of the conversation. Anderson had only heard the part where the sheriff said, "Come with me."

"Aunt Kit don't never use that ax." Anderson stated emphatically. "Why you gotta take her in?" he cried becoming more upset. "She don't know nothin! Dat's Chester's ax!"

Sheriff Phillips turned and looked at Anderson. "What you know about it, boy?" he asked.

"I know dat Chester is da one dat uses dat ax!" he stated. "And when he ain't usin it Will Hawkins uses dat ax fo Mama." he said glaring at Will.

"Well, I guess you best come with me too." The Sheriff retorted. "You can explain it all down at the station. We'll come back and talk to your Auntie."

Mariah, Frank and Georgia looked on as Sheriff Phillips led Anderson away. Georgia wept as they got into the automobile and she watched the sheriff drive off with her son. She was terrified that Anderson would inadvertently say something to get himself into deeper trouble. The three of them slowly walked back into the house to commiserate about the new developments.

It was mid-morning when Bud's wife, Josie, arrived from Taylor. She clutched a copy of the Tuesday morning newspaper in her hands. "Special Edition," it said. Hesitantly, she handed it to Mariah.

Mariah slumped down into the chair, as the headlines screamed at her.

"BLOODY AX TELLS TALE OF MASSACRE."

"Minden, LA. -- The ax[with]which John Nelson Reeves, his wife and their two children are believed to have been murdered in the home near here, Christmas night was found today by searchers about half a mile from the scene of the crime. It was covered with blood and matted hair. The sheriff and his deputies who searched the homes of some of the negroes held in jail as suspects reported they had found bloody clothing therein, but the belief is strong here that a white man was involved in the crime. Nine negroes are being held in jail as suspects. It is said that Mrs. Reeves recently received $2500 in the settlement of an estate and this, with the $500, which her husband kept in the house, is supposed to have furnished the motive for the murders. None of the money has been found."

"Good Lord!" Mariah groaned. It was the first official information she'd had about the killings. She had known nothing about any possible motive. In a way, she felt that it was proof that Chester was not involved. The details were too gruesome for anything Chester could have been involved in. Besides, they had searched her house and the premises thoroughly. They had found a pistol and told her about the ax. However, no money was found. Almost everyone around town owned a pistol or a shotgun. They would have surely found money if Chester had been involved, wouldn't they? Still, there was enough information to make her shiver. Chester had mentioned going to the Reeves. She also knew that old man Reeves owed Chester money. And what about the ax? Why was *her* ax at the murder scene? Still, she didn't think Chester had killed anyone. He would never hurt someone in such a vicious manner. Especially children. Chester loved children. But he might know something about it. She hoped that he would just cooperate with the Sheriff and tell them what he knew, if anything. They would see that he could never commit such a violent act. Then he would be home soon, and tell Mariah that it was all a mistake. They would find the monsters that did this, and Chester would be cleared!

However, Chester wasn't cooperating with the Sheriff. In fact, he had said nothing. Chester was sitting in jail as he witnessed several of his brothers, a few cousins, and a few friends being led to various cells. He wasn't surprised. He knew that by tonight, the jail would be packed. Any colored man in the Grove area was suspect and would be picked up. That would include any of them who had ever said more than two words to Reeves. He was right. By nightfall, a loud buzz could be heard throughout the jail. People were talking. But Chester decided to keep his mouth shut.

Chester had been grilled several times already. He felt like a Ping-Pong ball being knocked around the table. Their tactics weren't exactly kind. They were boisterous in giving him the third degree. The police seemed to have a lot of details. Some of those details could only have been provided by two people; Mark or Larkin.

Chester didn't expect that Henry Waller or Johnny Long would be picked up. It was becoming clearer that the two of them had tricked him, Mark and Larkin. Waller had seemed awfully confident that night. And Johnny had looked downright sheepish, like he knew more than he was letting on. Chester rehashed the night repeatedly in his head. It appeared to be a well-planned frame-up. The evidence would point directly to him.

The pistol found between Chester's mattresses belonged to Mr. Reeves, and the ax belonged to his mother. That would explain why Henry Waller would give him the pistol and wanted him to bring the ax.

Sheriff Phillips walked up to Chester's cell again. The look on his face was grim. His eyes were red. His whole body shook with anger as stood in front of Chester.

"You best come clean now, Boy!" Phillips thundered at him. "Alto didn't make it! Now we got a fifteen month old baby dead!" His voice was cracking as he gave Chester the information.

"Did you hear me, boy?" he shouted. "That child is dead. And a white woman is dead. And we have an ax that says you killed em." He bellowed. "Things will be better for you if you just go on and confess. We already know what happened, boy. Just tell me why! Why did you do it?"

Chester was stunned. Sheriff Phillips had questioned him repeatedly, and it was intense. However, it was never as intense as this. Chester felt certain that Phillips would enter his cell and put a bullet in his head!

Sheriff Phillips took a couple of deep breaths to collect himself. He looked carefully at Chester who stood stunned and mute in the cell. Phillips lowered his voice and went back into detective mode. He wrung his hands together and continued.

"Ok. You don't want to talk? Well let me tell *you* what happened!" he said pulling up a nearby chair. We know that you, Mark, and Larkin and a couple of your brothers went over to the Reeves on Christmas Eve. We know that you boys robbed Mr. Reeves and hacked up everybody in the house!" His voice was strong again and rising to a crescendo. "Mrs. Reeves saw what happened and she ran for the door. But she had seen too much and you needed to silence her. So you grabbed Mr. Reeves pistol and chased her outside and around to the back of the house. Then you shot her point-blank in the head, but that wasn't enough. She didn't die quick enough for you! So you got that ax and you finished the job!" he accused.

Chester was badly shaken. Phillips did indeed have most of the story pieced together. The facts were pretty much on target, but there was a big problem. Chester wasn't the one who'd swung that ax! Moreover, there seemed to be major omissions. There was no mention of Henry Waller and Johnny Long. And other "facts" were way off base in that none of his brothers was even there.

Phillips stared at Chester for what seemed like an eternity. He studied him looking for a reaction. He wanted to see how Chester digested this bit of information. Phillips had dangled the rope. All he needed was for Chester for confirm his theory and fill in the blanks. Then they could be charged, tried and convicted.

Chester looked down. His brother, Bud's advice swirled around in his head. "Don't say a mumblin' word!" Bud had cautioned. Chester knew that Bud was right. Who would believe him? Henry had covered his tracks well and there wasn't even a hint of Henry and Johnny in the mix. Yep. It was best to heed Bud's advice and see how things shook out over the next few days. His eyes stayed fixed on the ground. "I don't know what you talkin' bout." he finally said.

Phillips angrily walked away. He was outraged that Chester was still refusing to say anything. Even with all of the evidence that had been placed before him, Chester did not attempt to deny, confirm or correct any of it. He would have to find a new way to get him to confess.

Chester figured that Mark and Larkin had spilled their guts. Phillips had too many details. They were probably afraid of the lynch mob. There seemed to be enough evidence to hang them, so maybe they talked. But if they had, why didn't Sheriff Phillips mention Henry or Johnny? No, Chester would wait it out. He didn't see the point in talking. If he told them what had happened, they wouldn't believe him anyway, so why talk? In a way, he was surprised that he was still alive, especially with the news that the baby had died.

He thought about the evidence against him that was continuing to pile up. Tracks of blood led directly from the Reeves door to his. He had Reeves pistol, and apparently Mrs. Reeves had been shot with it. The ax used in the killings belonged to his family. And there was a possibility of confessions from Larkin and Mark. Yes, Waller might be a drunk, but he had covered his tracks well. Waller knew that people wouldn't believe any colored folks over any white folks and he used that to his advantage. He was probably sitting in a big comfortable chair, grinning that evil grin of his and enjoying holiday leftovers while Chester sat in the cold, damp, and musty cell, waiting for the bars to open. He expected that any moment now the white folks would drag him out and string him up on the nearest tree.

He ran through the scenario in his head. It would be the dead of night. The Klan would storm the jailhouse and pull him kicking and screaming to the woods, or a swamp. They would ignore his cries and lead him to a remote area and hang him from a tree. Maybe they would chop up his body and dump him in the river.

Chester lay down on the cold lumpy cot and tried to get the images out of his head. No such luck. His situation only seemed to get more and more dire. One day in that jailhouse had seemed like a lifetime. So far, he had not been formally charged. But he knew that it didn't matter. Sheriff Phillips already believed that he was guilty. He would be charged soon. He would be convicted and he would be hung. And it was very likely that the hanging would come before the charge or the conviction.

Later that evening, Sheriff Phillips returned with two of his deputies. He motioned for one of them to open the cell. As Chester heard the keys turn in the lock, his heart raced and images of the Klan once more flashed before his eyes. He was certain that they were taking him to his death.

The deputies walked into his cell. Immediately, they handcuffed and shackled him. He could barely walk with the heavy chains gripped around his ankles. They half-dragged him out of the cell. He was reluctant to go. The sound of the keys dangling on the deputy's waist made him wish that he could grab them and lock himself back in the safety of his jail cell. He heard the heavy door clang shut behind him, and remembered that hollow sound from when he was first brought in. They had pushed him inside and the next thing he heard was that heavy iron door clanking shut behind him signaling the depth of his situation. The sound echoed in his head as he moved along.

But now, he felt that he was facing something worse than the jail cell. If they were taking him out of jail in the dead of night, it could only mean one thing. They were going to take him to his execution!

When they got to the steps outside of the jailhouse Chester looked around. He was surprised to see dozens of armed guards surrounding the place. There were reporters milling about, walking up to the guards and trying to get them to talk. Their pencils were poised over their tablets as they jotted down tidbits of information. And there was a mob! A group of deputies held a large angry mob at bay, a short distance from the jailhouse.

Suddenly, some of the members of the press spotted a handcuffed and heavily shackled Chester and rushed towards him. Chester flinched, fearful of the growing sea of white faces. They shouted questions at Chester and at the Sheriff from a distance.

"Did you hack the Reeves family to death with an ax?"

"Were you the ringleader of the group?"

"Are you afraid you'll be lynched?"

"Why did you pick Christmas Eve for the crime?"

"Was robbery the motive…?"

The press followed Chester and the deputies as closely as they could, shouting questions at them as they quickly moved along.

Chester held his head low as the heavy chains weighted his body down. Taking tiny steps, he shuffled towards the waiting police car. Sheriff Phillips pushed Chester's head underneath the rear car door and shoved him down into the seat. Then he strolled around to the driver's side and slid behind the wheel, nodding to the deputy who was on the passenger's side in the front.

Chester felt like his chest was going to explode as he contemplated their next move.

"Where are they taking me?" he thought. "The lake? A tree? Are they turning me over to the Klan?"

They drove past the armed guards and turned onto the bumpy road. It was dark and Chester could not see where they were heading.

"You sure you don't want to talk now, Boy?" Sheriff Phillips asked. "You want to try and save your sorry black ass and tell us what happened?" The deputy glared at him as the sheriff continued to berate him. As they moved down the road, Sheriff Phillips decided to change his strategy a bit.

"Chester, I been knowing your family a long time." Phillips said, lowering his voice. "Now we know some of the story, but we think somebody might be telling tales on you. We don't think you done it. At least not most of it. But we think you know something about it. The sooner you tell us who did this, the better it will be for you."

Chester looked up. "Sheriff, I don't have anything to tell you." Chester stated. "I don't know what happened to them people." Then he remembered his vow to keep silent. He weighed his options in his mind. He could lie and deny knowing anything about it. But that would lead to more questions. He would need to explain about the gun, the footprints, and the ax. His answers would lead to more questions. He considered telling them the truth about Henry, Johnny, and the others. He could tell them that Henry used his ax. He could explain how Henry forced them to go and then framed them. But he quickly changed his mind about telling. If they put him against the two white men, Henry would just lie and blame him. Henry would deny even being there. And Johnny would back Henry. And who would the law believe? "They would obviously believe the white men!" he thought. Hell! Mark and Larkin had obviously blabbed. They had probably told about Johnny and Henry. And they might be dangling from a rope by now. Chester thought he might be headed for the same fate. So, he just kept quiet.

Finally, the Sheriff and the deputy seemed to give up on him. They stopped questioning him and continued to make their way down the road. The drive seemed awfully long to Chester. "Maybe they're going to make sure my body is never found." He silently reasoned.

Abruptly, the automobile came to a halt. Chester peered out the window, expecting to be surrounded by trees. Instead, he was surrounded by large stone buildings. Sheriff Phillips got out of the car and walked around to the passenger side. He yanked Chester from the automobile and Chester took in his surroundings, thankful to breathe the fresh air. He recognized the area. He gazed over at the Caddo Parish courthouse. With a start, he realized what was to the left of the courthouse. It was the Caddo Parish Jail. He remembered seeing the new jailhouse built about ten years ago.

"Let's go, boy!" Sheriff Phillips pulled Chester along the walk. Trying to regain his balance in his shackles, he quickened his step, and the guards led him inside of the jail and up the stairs.

"Here's your new home, boy." The deputy said as he threw Chester into the cell. Once again, the sound of the bars clanging shut echoed as the heavy door was firmly locked. Chester didn't know whether to be relieved or distressed. He wasn't swinging from a rope. However, he was still locked up. They'd called it his new home. That sounded like a permanent condition. He went over to the bare cot and slumped down on it. There he lay, tossing and turning all night long.

The room grew brighter with the morning sun. Chester's thoughts turned to his family, reflecting particularly on his mother. Did she believe that her son was a killer? Had more of his brothers been arrested? Were they being harassed? Beaten? He knew that no one could visit him yet because the law allowed for holding a suspect up to 5 days without charging him. During that, time suspects were not allowed any visitors. But even if visits had been allowed, he didn't expect anyone to come. Hell, they probably wouldn't even know where he was, now.

Mariah faced her own set of problems at home. Neighbors and the press, hungry for story, surrounded her house day and night. She had not left the house since Christmas day for fear that an angry mob wanting revenge would be lying in wait right outside her door. She lived in constant fear for herself and her children. Her home had become her prison. The children could no longer play outside. Chores went undone around the property. A permanent knot rested in the pit of her stomach and made her feel like she needed to vomit.

There was no end to the questions. Mariah had no answers. She only knew what she heard from others.

Johari Ade

CHAPTER 6

INTERROGATION

Mariah had managed to piece together bits and pieces of the story from neighbors who recounted various newspaper reports. There was plenty of press. The news had been picked up by the Associated Press and was distributed far and wide. Mariah was astounded by the speed by which far-away places picked up the stories, and spinned them to their liking. Reporters from all of the adjoining states, and even as far away as Colorado and New Mexico seemed to have gotten ahold of the story. One of the neighbors brought over a newspaper one day and Mariah was shocked by what it said:

"NEGROES NAME WHITE MEN IN KILLING OF FAMILY"

Minden. La. Three negroes, Chester Tyson, Mark Peters and Larkin Stewart, held as suspects in the connection with the killing of 5 members of the John Nelson Reeves family, nine miles north of here early Christmas morning have confessed according to the county officers, implicating two white men, Henry Waller, a farmer and neighbor of Reeves and John Long, a 20-year-old youth. Long, it is said also has made a confession, declaring Waller instigated the crime with an ax, killing Reeves, his wife and three children. Friends of Waller, however, assert that he was in Serepta the night of the crime…

"Oh, my God!" Mariah exclaimed. "They gonna lynch my boys!" Mariah was alarmed by these new revelations. Being accused of murder was bad enough. But implicating a white man, especially one with an alibi, could mean a quick death. Mariah had seen too much over her 56 years. From where she stood, a black man's life wasn't worth two cents when placed next to the life of a white man. And this time there was a white woman and children in the mix. Just looking at a white woman could get you lynched. Being accused of killing one was unconscionable. Mariah feared that her sons would not make it in jail another day. She hoped that they would somehow be able to escape and get out of town. It would be better never to see her boys again, as long as she knew that they were alive and safe.

Mariah wasn't the only one who was concerned for their safety. Chester knew that the next day wasn't promised in light of the Reeves murders. Sitting in his cell at the Caddo Parish jailhouse, Chester jumped as he heard the keys jangling near the bars. The door opened and Sheriff Hughes and two deputies entered the cell. At the sight of the shackles and cuffs they were holding, Chester braced for what was to come. One of the deputies snatched him by the shoulder, turned him around and spread-eagled him against the wall. Chester knew the drill by now. He was going for a "walk." A different Sheriff would do the asking, but the interrogation would begin again.

They walked him down the hall sat him down in one of the offices. Chester noticed a newspaper on the desk. He rested his eyes on the boldly printed headlines:

"NEGROES TELL OF 5 MURDERS"

"Minden, LA., Two negroes held as suspects in connection with the killing of five members of the family of John Nelson Reeves have confessed, the police say, implicating Henry Waller...."

Chester strained his neck to see more but that was as far as he got before Sheriff Hughes turned around and noticed Chester looking at the paper. He yanked him out of the chair and led him down the hall to the interrogation room leaving him there. Chester paced back and forth in the interrogation room wondering what the headlines meant. "How much had they said!?" he wondered about Larkin and Mark. Finally, the sheriff returned.

"Come on, Boy! You're going for a little ride."

"Once more he was spirited out of the jailhouse and into a waiting automobile. They drove about three miles to a waiting train. Two deputies joined Chester onboard the train, taking seats on either side of him. The train was the Texas and Pacific Westbound train. He was headed away from Louisiana and towards Texas! As the train moved along, Chester didn't speak but the deputies riding with him were very talkative. Chester was certain that most of the conversation that they let "drop" was for his benefit. White people had a way of thinking that negroes were stupid. They would say things in front of you, obviously just to gauge your reaction, but you weren't supposed to recognize the scam. They were unmistakably doing that now, pretending to talk to each other but slyly keeping an eye on Chester to see if they could get a reaction out of him.

"You know that simple-minded boy?" the first deputy was saying in a loud whisper. "He confessed to them ax murders."

"Oh, you mean that young white kid, Johnny Long?" the second deputy offered. "Oh yeah! He confessed all right. But he lied when he said that Henry …"

Out of the side of his eye, Chester noticed the first deputy tense his back and try to redirect the conversation.

"I wasn't talkin about *him*!" the other deputy quickly interrupted him and jerked his head around to see if Chester was listening. "I was talking about Anderson Heard. That Negro kid!" The deputy was clearly agitated. He did not intend for the news about Johnny's confession to come out just yet, but it was too late. Now Chester knew that the suspicion might be pointed at someone else.

"Amateurs!" Chester thought to himself. They need to go back to police training school and learn how get their plans together before trying to reel in a suspect. Chester played it cool. He was listening. But he didn't let on that he was listening. Most troubling was the reference that they had made to "the negro Heard."

"Andy?" Chester thought. "Andy don't know nothing. "Why would they be talking about him?"

"The Negro Heard told us all about what him and the other Negroes did." The second deputy reiterated, still seething.

He was very angry at the first deputy. "If Chester realized that the finger was pointed at someone else, he might not talk at all." He hoped that Chester had not noticed the slip.

"Oh, yeah, I heard that the Negro Heard confessed!" the other deputy conceded, his face turning red from his obvious blunder. He finally realized his mistake. He knew that Chester shouldn't be made aware that there was another possible person on whom to blame the murder. Especially a white person. The idea was to make him think that all things pointed to him, so that he confessed. Chester had heard. But he kept his eyes fixed on the trees and buildings that they passed and kept a straight face. Nevertheless, for the first time in a long time, he felt somewhat hopeful. If Johnny had an attack of conscience and told the law about Henry, they might be saved. Johnny might be young and a little "green." But he was white. And a white boy could do something that black men could not. He could sway the jury against other white criminals. And a white boy would be believed over any of the colored men.

Chester wasn't too worried about Anderson.

"Andy doesn't know anything." he reasoned. "They won't hold him long.

Chester was deep in thought when the train slowed towards the next stop.

"Next stop --Texarkana!" The conductor called. "All passengers for Texarkana, Arkansas, or Texarkana, Texas, please gather your belongings."

Chester had been to Texarkana several times. In fact, his brother Sing Tyson lived there. He wished he could see him. He was sure that Sing would know about his plight by now. But he was certain that his brother would not even know he was in Texarkana. Everyone probably thought that he was still in the Webster County jailhouse.

Chester was thrown into a small dank cell. He looked around, taking in his new surroundings. He flung himself down on the bottom cot and stared at the walls, pondering his fate. The new developments were interesting. He didn't put any stock in the things that the sheriff or deputies let "slip" while he was in their presence. But he had gotten a peek at the newspaper. They probably didn't attempt to hide the newspaper from him because they thought he couldn't read. It reminded him of the time they asked his uncle to mark an "X" because they assumed he couldn't write. They never realized that his uncle could read and write and was in fact a prominent preacher in the colored community.

The newspaper had confirmed that Henry Waller had been implicated. And if Henry Waller was implicated, that meant that Johnny Long had talked. It had to be Johnny because the law wouldn't give any credence to a negro blaming a white man. Hell, even though Johnny might have been in on it with Waller, he looked like he was gonna jump out of his skin on the night of the killings. He didn't really look like he wanted to be there any more than Chester and the others did. Nevertheless, Chester didn't expect Johnny to say too much, or turn against Henry. Henry would kill Johnny just as soon as look at him. But Johnny was a kid. He was apparently a very scared kid. It wouldn't take much for the sheriff to get him to tell all he knew. This new development might prove to be favorable to Chester.

He was still deep in thought when the heavy iron bars opened and the deputy arrived with another prisoner.

"Here we are Ellis. Get in there, boy!" the deputy said to the prisoner. "You may as well make yourself comfortable cuz you gonna be here a good while." He said while pushing him into the cell and clanking the bars shut behind him.

"Oh, Hell!" Chester thought. "I don't want no roommate. "I hope this guy just keeps to himself." Chester wasn't looking forward to being chatty with anyone. He needed time to think.

He glanced at his cellmate out of the corner of his eye. The guy climbed up on the top bunk and wordlessly stared at the ceiling for about five minutes. He finally spoke.

"Ain't this some mess?" he began. "Being in this stankin cell for some stupid shit. I reckon they'll keep me in here till they send my ass to the Pen. Guilty until proven innocent, I say." You know how it goes!" he stated emphatically.

Then Ellis held his breath, waiting for Chester to reply. He didn't want to give too much away about what he was actually doing there so he decided to take it slow. His name wasn't really "Ellis". And he wasn't really a prisoner. His name was Will, and he was a black detective, employed by the Price Brothers Detective Agency in Shreveport. He was there as a confidential informant. His task was to get Chester to confess.

He knew he had to be careful. Some colored men that knew him well told him that he looked like the law and smelled like the law. However, he knew that if he played his cards right that he could get Chester to talk. Chester wasn't talking to the sheriff or any of the other deputies. They felt that Chester needed someone "of his own kind" to trust and get him to open up. Sometimes Will felt bad about tricking other colored men into talking, but not this time. If Chester did murder all of those people, he deserved to rot in hell. And Will wouldn't mind helping to put him away for good.

"Ellis" kept complaining about the injustice of it all until Chester felt that he had to respond.

"What you in here for?" Chester finally asked his cellmate. He didn't really care, but he didn't want to be out right rude by remaining silent.

"They is saying I robbed a bank and shot two deputy sheriffs." "Ellis" offered. "But they got the wrong man. I was right by that bank and a gunshot came whizzin' right by my ear. Next thang I know, two deputies is down and a pistol is lying right at muh feet. I was just standin there, that's all. But it weren't my gun. Somebody else dropped it and ran with all the ruckus going on. It musta landed by my feet. But you know how the law is around here. Pick up every nigger in sight and jail em all. Figure it out later." He finished. The plan had been to tell Chester that he had actually robbed a bank, but he decided to switch it up at the last minute. "Ellis" figured that he would get more information and sympathy if the played the "innocent" routine.

"Anybody die?" asked Chester.

"Yeah, man! Both them white deputies is dead!"

"Then your ass is going down!" Chester offered. "If it woulda been a colored man you wouldn't have nothin' to worry about. But a white man and a deputy at that? Your ass is going down!" he repeated.

"But they already had it out for me" 'Ellis' continued. Now that

Chester was talking, he wanted to keep the conversation going. "They's always on my ass bout something! They think I robbed a white woman last year. But they couldn't pin it on me cuz I was in town wit black folk *and* white folk. But some still want to see me hang. And this here is their chance." He finished.

"You's probably right" Chester agreed. He slumped back into the cot, seemingly finished with the conversation.

"Ellis" contemplated his next move. He wanted to size Chester up to see what made him "tick." Chester didn't seem to be as closed-mouth as Sheriff had led him to believe. It was just as he thought. Chester hadn't talked because he didn't want to talk to white folks. He understood that way of thinking. He used to think that way himself until he had gotten to know some good white folks who treated him fairly. But he could work with that.

It was important to impress upon Chester that he understood the racism surrounding them. He would show how he understood that negroes were automatically suspect when a crime was committed. Will knew all about the case, and about fingers being pointed to Johnny and Waller as well as Chester and the others. He would play the part of a victim, to get Chester to talk. He reasoned that if he appeared to be a victim too, then Chester would open up.

Nevertheless, Chester remained silent about the crime.

"This isn't going to be as easy as I thought," Ellis surmised. He tried several times to turn the conversation to Chester's crime. However, Chester said very little other than to say he was innocent too.

The cell took on a gloomy look as dusk stole the light. As the guard slipped dinner through the meal slot "Ellis" realized that he would be locked up with Chester for the night. He didn't relish spending an entire Sunday night in the cold cell, but he figured that it might work to his advantage. He didn't think it wise to press Chester too far, too fast. A good night's sleep might make him more talkative. So, he backed off for a while and made more small talk.

Somewhere in between his talking about fishing and talking about women, he heard Chester snoring softly on the bottom bunk. "Oh, Hell!" he thought. "I can't wake him up now. That would just make him suspicious. I'll try again in the morning." He tossed and turned on the tiny cot trying to find a comfortable position. He periodically nodded off and then awakened with a start, realizing he was locked up with a man accused of murder.

They awoke the next day to the smell of coffee in the air. It was a Monday morning, and a lot noisier than it had been the day before. Soon they heard feet shuffling towards their cell.

"Here's your hot biscuits and scrumptious steak, piping hot and cooked just like you ordered it!" the guard said as he pushed the cold biscuits and gravy, and the lumpy grits through the slot in the bars. Amused at his own joke, he headed towards the next cell.

Chester and "Ellis" made small talk for the next hour or so while they delved into the biscuits and gravy, and lukewarm coffee. With Chester's belly full, "Ellis" found an opening where he thought that he might be able to steer the conversation back to the crime.

"What you say you in here for?" He finally asked Chester, trying to sound casual.

"I told you. For somethin' I ain't done." Chester answered. "They think I killed somebody."

"Oh, man!" Ellis stated. Sounds like you got yo'self in a heap of trouble. What'd they say when you explained it to em'?" he asked.

"I ain't tried to explain nothin." Chester answered. "For what? They don't want to hear what I have to say."

"Yeah, man, I know what you mean." Ellis said. "They think they already know everything. But you gotta make sure they know your side of it, or they'll make up their own story." He cautioned. He figured that he would nudge Chester, but not push him. That way he could gain his trust. He would get more information that way, he reasoned. He couldn't let on that he was "pumping" him for information. But once again, Chester had stopped talking.

"Man, oh Man. I sho miss my girl!" Ellis stated about twenty minutes later. "I know she's settin up there wondering if I'm ever gonna come back. I got two kids too. I sho hope they get this mess straightened out!" he anguished.

Chester did begin to relax a little. He was glad he didn't have a lunatic or some drunk throwing up all over him. And he could relate to what Ellis was saying about family. It made him think of his own family.

"Well, I ain't gonna neva see my family no mo'" Chester said sadly. "But you – you maybe got a little chance. There was other people 'round you. They might figure it out. But me? Ain't nobody gonna believe me!"

"Why you think that?" "Ellis" said, hoping that he didn't sound too anxious. He was pretty sure that he had laid the foundation for Chester to confess. He just needed to bide his time.

"Because some jack-ass set it up that way." Chester replied, shaking his head. "They's sayin' that I killed some white people." He said finally. "But I ain't done what dey sayin I did."

Will took a deep breath. There it was! This was the moment of truth! Chester was talking. Now all he had to do was plant the right questions here and there and let him talk.

"But why they think you had somthin to do wit it?" "Ellis" asked.

Chester hesitated. He had really tried to keep it all in. But it was weighing heavy on his heart. At the same time, it felt good to get it off his chest. "Because dats what that cracker wanted em to thank!" Chester retorted. "That cracker done framed me and I cain't do a damn thing about it!" he cried.

"What Cracker?" Will asked. "Somebody you knew?"

"Yeah. I knew him" he said.

Chester seemed somewhat relieved once he started talking. The week in jail seemed like an eternity. He felt like his head was going to explode from keeping everything pent up inside. It felt good to finally let it go.

"I had just got home and all I wanted was a good night's sleep." He started.

Ellis took a deep breath. It sounded like Chester was going to start at the beginning. That meant that he would have all the information he needed for his boss.

"Man, it was Christmas Eve!" Chester said incredulously. "I was s'posed to get married on Christmas day! I'd been out havin' a good time with my girl up at the Juke Joint. I was high as a kite so I goes home, right? I was feeling good. I can still smell that peach cobbler that was settin on the stove when I opened that door. I was getting ready to go to bed and I hears this knockin at the door. I open up the damn door and this drunk ass cracker, Henry Waller is standin there talkin about, "Let's go play some cards!"

"Did you go?" Ellis asked.

"I finally did." Chester answered. "The man wouldn't take 'no' for an answer. I thought that he was gonna wake Mama up and Mama hates that man!" he stated emphatically. "And you know how them crackers are. They ain't really asking ya. They's tellin ya. When they say jump you supposed to ask "how high?"

"I know what you mean!" Ellis agreed. "They don't expect no less!"

Chester was in a zone now. It was as if he was reliving that night.

The night that changed everything!

"Anyways, I knew he weren't gonna give up. And I was afraid he'd wake up Mama and the kids. So, I went with him. I thought I could make some excuse and get back home soon after we gits there. Then he stops by my cousins house, cuz he says we needs at least four men to play. Man! I shoulda know'd something was wrong when he wanted me to bring muh ax!"

"Your ax?" Ellis inquired. Now they were getting somewhere. Chester was finally talking about the ax!

"Yeah. My ax was settin in a stump. Waller saw it and mumbled some sorry-ass excuse about using it to clear some brush through a shortcut. But the trail is pretty clear all around. I figured he jest wanted it for hisself." Chester showed no sign of stopping. He was just at the beginning but "Ellis" knew the rest would come.

"Anyways, when we gets to my cousin's house, they's another colored fella and a white kid comin' with us. Now I'm thinkin that's good cause they's more than four of us to gamble and I can leave as soon as they's all settled.

"So we gets up to the house and alla the lights is off. I'm thinkin dat deys sleep and now we can go home. But that's when that Cracker starts actin all crazy. He said we was gonna go in and wake em up. He starts barkin out orders and then I knowed for sho that he was up to no good. He snatches the ax from me and tells me to stand guard by the house. Man, there was evil in his eyes like I aint never seen before. He looked like he was ten feet tall when he had dat ax. And I know'd that he'd a hit me wit it if I crossed him. So I stayed put." Chester stopped talking. He had almost forgotten that anyone else was with him. He was deep in thought, reliving that night. He was back in the midst of that hellish experience. And he didn't want to relive the next moments. He wanted to forget. At the same time, telling about it was cathartic. It was as if he was explaining it to himself. In speaking about that night, he was able to gain clarity about some things that made little sense at the time that they happened.

"Ellis" began to worry that Chester wouldn't get to the main part of the story. What exactly had happened inside of that house? He knew he had to give Chester a nudge to keep him talking.

"So was anybody still up?" he gently prodded.

"Up? No, warn't nobody up." Chester said, remembering the dimly lit room and the light from the fireplace. "The house was dark, cept you could see a little light through some cracks in da house because the fireplace was lit up and an oil lamp musta been on in da house somewheah. Man, as soon as I stepped in that doorway, I saw in da bedroom. And dey was somebody layin on that bed. Musta been Mistah Reeves. Henry lifted dat ax and 'bamm!' dat ax came down on dat bed and then…." Chester's voice cracked and trailed off, remembering the next moments of pure hell.

"Then Waller hit him! He hit him with dat ax. Man I ain't never been so scared in my life! He kepta swinging that ax! I was sho dat I was next and as good as dead. But sumpin caught his attention in the next room and he ran right past me. Man, I'm tellin you….." Chester's voice trailed off. He took a deep breath. His heart was pounding in his chest. Beads of perspiration dotted his forehead. He'd finally told the story. He had said it out loud and gotten it off his chest.

"Ellis" looked up at the ceiling, taking it all in. He had become so engrossed in the details that he almost forgot that he was there on assignment. He believed Chester. He heard the pain and distress in his voice. It had affected him. He was perplexed at how anyone could do such a thing. He understood how Chester could believe himself to be Waller's next victim if he didn't do as he was told. It explained everything that he had heard about the crime. Nevertheless, he had a job to do. He had to get the rest of the story. Chester's story had explained John Reeves death. But what about the children? What about Mrs. Reeves? After taking a deep breath, he spoke, gently guiding Chester to reveal more of the details.

"Man, I know you musta been glad to get outa there." Will stated. "Did he run after you?"

"No." Chester said putting his head in his hands. "I was so glad to jest be outa there that I stopped to catch my breath. But it happened so fast! There was a bunch of noises and scuffling and stuff coming outa dat house. Then that door flew open and Henry was chasin' Miss Maudie down the steps and around back. She was a runnin, and a yellin and a hollerin. Then all of a sudden, I hears a gunshot. Then it got real quiet and I knowed he shot her."

"He just up and shot the woman?" Ellis was astonished.

"Dat's what I figure. A second later, Henry comes walkin' back actin' like ain't nothin' happen. He was still waving that ax around and I thought I was a dead man. I thought he was gonna shoot me when he pointed dat gun in my direction! Then he says, "You take this! And he gives me old man Reeves pistol like it's some kinda reward or somethin'. Then my dumb ass takes it home. After I gits home and thought about it for awhile, I knowed that Cracker set us up!" Chester finished.

"Ellis" had listened to the whole story. He'd done what he had come to do. However, it didn't quite turn out as he had expected. He had come into the job very angry at Chester. Not only for killing the children and their family but because he felt that Chester had made it hard for all of the other colored men in their town. White folks weren't just mad at Chester and the others in jail, they were mad at any colored man who walked the streets. That's the way it was. Whenever a colored man robbed somebody or attacked somebody, they all paid the price for it. That was one reason that he had gone into the detective business. He wanted to prove that colored men were decent, law-abiding human beings. When he thought that Chester had committed the crime, he was glad to do his part to get the vicious criminal locked up. Now he had to go back to Mr. Price and tell him that although he had succeeded in getting Chester to talk, that Chester had denied doing the crime. He would tell Mr. Price what Chester had said. He figured that there was a chance that Chester was lying, but he believed him. On the other hand, Mr. Price had been so convinced that Chester was guilty that he just might think that "Ellis" didn't question Chester good enough. He might think that Chester saw through him and lied to him. He really hoped that Price wouldn't think that he was just unwilling to send a colored man to prison. They weren't expected to "turn" on each other. "Like sticks with like," was the general sentiment in Louisiana. What that meant was that if you were black, you most likely protected your own and if you were white, you did the same. Now his task was to get Chester to tell the Sheriff exactly what happened. That was not going to be easy. But given the details he really felt that they might go easy on Chester if he told them the whole story. After all, Chester only went along because he was forced to.

Chester's confession had also put "Ellis" in a terrible position. He would have to go back and tell his boss that Chester, like the other black men, was pointing the finger at two white men. He knew that it would not be well received. But his mission had simply been to get Chester to confess to the authorities. And he had already succeeded in getting him to talk.

"Ellis" jumped down off the top bunk and stood near Chester. He wanted Chester to know that he believed him. He wanted him to know that his story made sense. He felt in his heart that he could help Chester, but he needed Chester to look into his eyes so that he knew that he was sincere.

"Look, Man," Ellis stated. "You got to tell em what happened! You got all those other people who was there that know'd you ain't done it. Why don't you just go to the Sheriff and tell it to him straight?" he suggested.

"Nigga are you crazy?" Chester retorted. "Think about it. I'm a dead man whether I tell em or not! They ain't gonna believe no nigger."

"But this time it's different." Will insisted. "Kids are involved. A white man's been hacked up, and a white woman was shot." They're jest gonna want the bastard who done it -- black or white. They just want to put away whoever done it." He repeated.

"Besides, that white boy was there and he saw the whole thing." He can back up your story."

"He ain't gonna back up nothin." Chester said sadly. "Johnny ain't gonna say nothing against that man. Waller said he'd kill us if *any* of us talk. Naw, Johnny's gonna be too scared to cross Waller."

"Maybe not." Will pressed, not wanting to let on that Johnny had already confessed. "Maybe when they question him he'll be afraid of spending the rest of his life in prison. Even if he lies they gonna see right through it cause he just a kid." Ellis insisted.

Chester paused thoughtfully. "Ellis" knew that he was considering talking to the Sheriff. All he needed was a few more words of encouragement.

"Look at it this way," he pressed. "If they really thought you done it, yo' ass would be strung up already. But you's still here. That right there says a lot. You ain't got nothing to lose by tellin em the truth."

Chester gave it some serious thought. He remembered the sheriff saying that they were moving him to keep him from the lynch mob. If they really thought he was a murderer they would have probably let the Klan have at him. Then there was the question of Larkin and Mark. From the little snippet he saw in the paper and the questions that the Sheriff had asked, Chester knew that they had already talked. For all he knew, they might have blamed him for all of it. He might be better off telling his own story.

Nevertheless, he knew that the color of his skin would be the overriding factor. He thought of his mother, Mariah and her assertion that "it's always about race." He thought about his brother Bud's admonition to "not say a mumbling word." He had probably already said too much." He remembered his cousin strung up and dangling from the end of a rope despite his assertions of innocence. Nope. He'd better keep quiet. "I ain't tellin em nothing!' he stated flatly. "They ain't never gonna believe it."

"Ellis" hung his head. He had done his best. The day was nearing its end. He couldn't let on that he was undercover but tomorrow he would let it be known that his work was done. Price wouldn't like the fact that Chester had implicated Henry Waller as the killer. Nevertheless, Chester's story collaborated Johnny Long's story. And Johnny Long was white. To avoid suspicion he would finish out the night in the jail, and leave in the morning.

The smell of coffee greeted them the next morning. The heavy shuffling of feet could be heard down the hall as the guards made their rounds. "Ellis" glanced anxiously at Chester, hoping that he had changed his mind about talking, but the guard came and went as Chester stared straight ahead, saying nothing. So, with the next round, Will gave the pre-arranged signal to let the guard know that his work was done.

"Come on Ellis!" the guard announced as he jangled his keys. You are headed to Penitentiary!"

Protesting just enough for effect, "Ellis" jumped down off the bunk and made his way out of the cell. The guard took him directly to Detective Price who was waiting in the interrogation room.

"Did he finally confess?" Price inquired excitedly as Will entered the room.

"Not exactly." Will shook his head slowly, fearing Price's reaction to his failure to secure the confession.

"Still ain't talkin, huh." Price sadly stated, certain that Chester had held hard and fast to his silence.

"Oh, he's talking!" Will answered. "But he is puttin' the finger on that white man-- Henry Waller. He is sayin' that Waller is the killer."

"He's blamin' Waller!?" Price was incredulous. "I knew that those other niggers were gonna try to frame him, but I thought that Chester might finally break down and tell the truth." He pounded his fist on the table, angry at this bit of news. Then he brightened a bit and looked up with a smile.

"But hey, no problem" Price said confidently. "Waller has an air tight alibi. We got Chester talking now, and I'm sure his statement is full of holes. Yeah, we got him now!" he finished excitedly. "So what did his sorry ass say?"

"He is saying that Henry Waller set him up. He admitted being at the house, but he says that Waller planned the whole thing and duped 'em."

"He said it all started when Henry come round to his house late on Christmas Eve. Said he didn't want to go but Henry threatened him with his shotgun."

"Now that's a bold-faced lie!" Price shouted.

"I don't know, Detective," Will said. "Way he told it, it all fit together." Will repeated Chester's story, careful not to omit any details. Detective Price was in disbelief. He didn't like what he heard. The story was almost exactly the same as the one told by Mark and Larkin, who were still being held. And that worried Detective Price. Chester's statement also collaborated the confession made by Johnny Long when Johnny had implicated Henry the day he was arrested.

"They are framing Waller!" Price bellowed. "Waller wasn't even there! He can prove it! Several reputable people came forward of their own free will and said that they saw him up in Serepta on Christmas Eve. That's twenty miles from Grove. He couldn't possibly have been in two places at the same time! That nigger is lying!" he repeated.

"But he told it so straight." Will said. "I really don't think he done it. Jest somethin' about the way he said it made me think that…."

"Don't you be fooled boy!" Price cautioned. "You think anybody that hacked up a whole family can't spin a good tale?" he asked. "As sure as the sun rose up this morning, he done it. And he's using *you* to carry the tale and frame Waller!"

Will said nothing. He believed Chester, but there was some truth to what Price said. How could Waller have been in two places at the same time? He wondered if Chester had confused another white man with Waller.

"And there's something else that come to light the other day." Price continued. "Chester's own cousin, Anderson Heard said that Chester used that ax and killed all those people. Why would the boy's own kin lie?" he asked. "He and Chester are blood! I'm gonna take this information to Detective Phillips up in Minden to see what he wants to do about it. Now you go on and just lay low until I get back to you. Don't tell nobody else about this, you hear?" he cautioned.

"No, Sir, I won't." Will agreed. He left the jailhouse, conflicted and confused. He had been so sure that Chester was telling the truth. But much of what Price said made sense. Chester could be lying through his teeth.

Detective Price picked up the keys to his automobile and headed out the door. He would deliver this latest bit of news to Sheriff Phillips in person. Now that Chester was talking, Price was certain that they could force him to repeat his confession to the authorities and then they could force him to admit to the murders. He just needed to make sure Phillips understood how cunning Chester Tyson could be. Phillips didn't understand the Negroes like Price did. After all, he worked with one!

Price knew that Sheriff Phillips didn't put too much weight on Anderson's confession because Anderson had changed his story a number of times. Many of the detectives who had interviewed Anderson said that he seemed to have a screw loose, but he seemed to know a lot about the crime. But Sheriff Hughes believed Anderson. And so did Price. He would impress upon Phillips that Negroes played dumb when it suited them. Anderson probably wanted to play as if he was dim so that if things got too hot, he could get out of it somehow. That wouldn't fly with Price. He had assisted with the case from the very beginning. He thought that it should be handed over to the grand jury for indictments at once.

When Price arrived at the Minden jail, Sheriff Phillips greeted him with some news of his own.

"We arrested Henry Waller." He announced sullenly.

"On what evidence?" Price was enraged. "His alibi checks out!"

"Yeah, but his alibi is too pat." Phillips said. "There is a big time gap between the time people saw him, and when the murders were committed. Henry had plenty of time between the time the last person says they saw him, and when the murders were committed."

"But they saw him in Serepta!" Price protested. "Do you know how far Serepta is from Grove? There is no way a man could get all the way from Serepta to Grove after midnight, murder five people, and be getting a shave in Serepta at eight o'clock the next morning!"

"It would be easy if they hired an automobile." Phillips responded. "When Johnny gave his confession, he said that Waller told him to hire a motor car. He said he couldn't get a motor car so he took his brother's horse. What's to say that Waller didn't hire a car?" he pointed out.

"We got Johnny's confession and it matches up with Mark's and Larkin's confession. And we got a timeline that fits." He stated.

Sheriff Phillips pulled out a sheet of paper and grabbed a pencil. "Come take a look." He said as he started to make a drawing on the paper.

"Now here is Serepta right here." He said drawing an "x." And Germantown where he lives is right here." He said making a second x." And here in the middle is Grove, and the Waller house sit's here." He said drawing a circle.

Sheriff Phillips continued to draw a sketch on his pad. He drew lines and put the distances between all the points on the paper. He drew little triangles indicating the homes of Chester, Mark, Larkin, Anderson, and Johnny. He drew a big red circle around the murder house. Then he held up his masterpiece for Detective Price to view.

"Ok, so Waller takes his horse and parades through town making sure that a bunch of people see him." Phillips continued, tracing his fingers over his sketch. "He stops and has a bite to eat, and picks up a present for his lady friend. He goes to bed and then sneaks back out after everybody is sleep. Then he walks over to an automobile that he has put in place earlier, with no one the wiser. He drives over to Grove and ditches the car in the woods. Then he walks to get the others. After the murders, he sends them off, gets back in his car and heads back to Serepta. Plenty of time to spare!" He finished.

"But you forgot something!" Detective Price protested. "We have a confession from Chester's own cousin. And as for the automobile, where is it?" he asked. "They all rode horses."

"You can ditch an automobile anywhere if nobody knows you got it." he insisted. "That time of night you can steal one and nobody would be the wiser. A horse is a live animal. They have to be accounted for. And a horse traveling forty miles over a few hours would show fatigue the next morning. Besides, not one person said they actually saw Waller riding a horse. They saw him in a wagon or on foot."

"That still doesn't explain Heard's confession." Price stated flatly.

"Heard is a nitwit!" Phillips bellowed. First, he was there and then he wasn't there. First Chester did it and then he didn't do it. You can't put no stock in Heard's story!" he insisted.

"Besides, the others all agree that Heard wasn't there, and there is no physical evidence that links him to the crime."

Detective Price was mum. "He's making a mistake," he thought to himself. However, he could see that Sheriff Phillips had his mind made up. He was sure that indictments against Waller would follow.

On the strength of Johnny's confession, Henry Waller was arrested and taken to the Mansfield Parish jail. And the only talking Waller was doing was to protest his innocence. The following day the headlines fueled the fire even further as the news hit the streets:

"CONFESSIONS OF 3 NEGROES ARE DOUBTED IN MINDEN"

Special to the times

   Minden, La, Dec 30 – People from all over the Parish have been in town and they have gathered in groups discussing the confessions of the [three] negroes and young Long, which implicated Waller as the ring-leader in committing the Crime... Many do not believe Waller is guilty. His friends say that they have absolute proof that Waller spent the night in which the murders were committed in Serepta... Harmon Drew, district attorney at Minden, has been in consultation with Sheriff Hughes, since the confessions and arrest and after reading the prisoners' statements announced that the physical evidence of the case absolutely corroborates the confessions...It has also been intimated at Minden that Long is more or less weak-minded and hardly responsible for what he might say when laboring under great excitement, as could have been induced by reading accounts of the murder and by all the comment it has occasioned...

The town was in an uproar. The case was ripping the community apart. People assembled all around town to discuss the new developments. They bemoaned the fact that their peaceful community was now in shambles. There was one thing upon which that they all agreed. A horrible crime had been committed and the people who did this should pay. They wanted blood. The only difference in opinion was exactly *whose* blood they wanted.

Henry Waller's family and friends were livid! How could the law have arrested Henry? Henry was part of a good, upstanding family. Besides, many of them had seen him with their own eyes shortly before the murders and they were convinced of his innocence. How could the law take the word of Negroes over a good, white, upstanding family? Henry's sons were demanding his release!

Three of John Nelson Reeves sons had arrived to oversee the burial of their father and nephews. It was a profound tragedy to bury an entire family. And the press wouldn't leave them alone. The papers painted Grove as a hate-filled racist place and the community resented it. However, the residents of Grove insisted that they just wanted justice. Black or white, they wanted to killers to pay.

But as details began to emerge, racial tensions continued to rise. The wrath of the white community was unleashed against the black community. Black men were viewed with suspicion and disgust wherever they went. Chester's, Mark's, Anderson's and Larkin's families were constantly under siege by the community and the press.

The day after Henry Waller's arrest Mariah opened the door to find one of her white neighbors standing on the other side of it. Although they warmly greeted each other in passing when the occasion arose, they were far from friends. However, the woman had come on behalf of the Grove neighborhood to deliver a message.

"Mariah, I know this can't be easy for you," she began. "We are not blaming you for what your son did. Lord knows that many of us have children who have gone astray. But I don't think that this town is safe for you anymore. I'm sure you've heard the threats from those outsiders. And frankly, some is sayin' that it is just too hard to have the family of a MURDERER living in our midst. We are prepared to purchase your land so that you can move to somewhere that would be better for you and your family. I'm sure that you agree. You don't want to be around here with everything that's going on. I know I wouldn't want to be here. So we are going to help you find someplace better.

"I appreciate your concern, Miss Martha, but we are gonna stay here and stick it out." Mariah said sadly. This has been our home for over 30 years. And I think that when people find out that Chester didn't do it, they will come around. It's just a matter of time before the truth comes out and our boys names will be cleared. Them boys couldn't have done that. You know that! They ain't got in in em."

"Well, I guess you know what's best." Martha sadly replied. "But just think about what I said. It ain't gonna be easy."

Mariah saw her to the door and she did indeed think about what she said. Mariah knew that the road ahead would be tough. Most of the blacks and whites in their small town were cordial to each other. Some of their children even played together. Nevertheless, people were becoming more and more divided because of the case. Many whites in the neighborhood were certain that the "niggers" were trying to frame

Henry Waller. Some believed Henry, Johnny, and "ALL of the negroes" were guilty. Many of the colored men in the community became fearful of traveling alone. However, they all agreed on one thing. They wanted peace and justice!

The grand jury adjourned the following week. Details were sketchy on what indictments they had handed down. Newspaper reports said that the Grand Jury had charged Chester, Mark, Larkin, and Anderson Heard with all of the murders. There were conflicting stories about whether or not Henry Waller and Johnny Long were charged. No trial date was announced. Mariah attempted to find the whereabouts of Chester, but failed to obtain any reliable information. She heard that the law had moved him several times to keep him from the lynch mob.

A few days later, she opened her door to find a newspaper laying on the step. It had a rubber band around it, and a crude drawing was tucked inside the rubber band. It was a drawing of a hooked cross with a red dot in the middle. Mariah immediately recognized it as a Klan emblem! Mariah threw the drawing aside and glanced down at the headlines in the paper. Her heart took a dive.

"Death Sentence Follows Trial of One Hour"

With her heart in her throat, Mariah began to read the article from the *Shreveport Times*.

"Texarkana, Ark. Jan 15. - John Hawkins, a negro, today was tried convicted and sentenced to be electrocuted all within an hour and a half, for the murder of Mrs. Ben Diles and her 18-month old daughter at Ashdown, Ark., in November... Hawkins confessed that he....."

Mariah took a deep breath. The newspaper article was about some-one else, --- not her son. She had heard of the Hawkins case and she was taken aback by the speed of his trial. She knew that swift hangings were not unusual for colored men in the South, especially in Louisiana and Mississippi. It was often the lynch mob who meted out the punishment. Mariah knew that Chester and the others might be headed for a similar fate. She was certain that the literature left at her door was a warning of some sort.

The following day, she was out in her front yard gathering wood when her nephew Adversus Heard arrived. Adversus was Anderson's older brother. With a troubled look on his face, he greeted her, "Mornin' Aunt Kit."

"Mornin' son." Mariah replied. "Everything ok?"

"I been called to testify." Adversus replied. "They wants me to tell what I know about Andy."

"Andy?" she asked. "What about Andy?"

"They come around questioning me the day after the killins. I told em what Andy said --- that he weren't ova there when those killins happen. He told me he was comin' ova heah to go to Chester's wedding I guess they want me to tell it to the Judge."

"They ask you anything about Chester?"

"Asked me what I knew. I tol' em I ain't seen Chester that day."

CHAPTER 7

PEOPLE VS CHESTER TYSON, ET. AL.

Mariah was deep in thought. She had heard nothing about a trial, but if Adversus had been summoned to court, it meant that the trial date was near. "Why had no one told her?" she wondered.

"The trial is day after tomorrow." Adversus answered her thoughts.

"Day after tomorrow?" she cried. "A trial? Already? Ain't nobody said nothing!" She was clearly distraught by the news. She was unprepared for this revelation.

She spent the rest of the day talking to her sisters and other family members about the trial. Although they all said the positive things to lift up each other, they all expected the worse.

January 29, 1917 was a crisp winter day. Word had gotten out about the trial, and people were milling about, excitedly discussing what was sure to be the trial of the century. Although some decided to make the trip to the Minden Courthouse, Mariah could not bring herself to go. She did not want to face the press, and the thought of Chester in chains brought tears to her eyes. She couldn't stand the thought of it. She would send a few of the men in the family and they would tell her what she needed to know.

Adversus, Leonard, and a few of their brothers headed up to the courthouse in Minden. When they arrived, they were taken aback by the number of armed guards surrounding the place. Apparently, the efforts by the authorities to keep the trial date a secret had failed. Dozens of people were arriving at the courthouse. The sheriff had not taken any chances though and apparently, they were ready for the large crowds. Adversus hesitated as he witnessed the deputies search each person before they entered the courthouse. He watched as one deputy removed a Barlow knife from a visitor's pocket as the man adamantly tried to convince the deputy that he was not out to harm the prisoners.

Finally, Adversus and the others stood before the deputy. Fortunately, the deputy recognized him as family and he ushered them in after a thorough searching. They took a seat in the back of the courtroom, a few rows behind several women who were attendance. Soon the courtroom was full, with white men sitting in the front rows. The women who were in attendance sat in the rear bench on one side, and the negroes who were in attendance sat in chairs in the rear on the other side.

As the courtroom filled, the buzz grew louder, and the spectators mounted a spirited debate about the merits of the case. They kept one eye on the side door, anxiously awaiting for the trial to begin.

Finally, Harmon Drew, the district attorney, followed by his deputy district attorney entered and made their way through the swinging doors in the front of the courtroom. Drew, having only been district attorney for a few months, strode confidently over to the prosecution's table. He nodded a cordial greeting to a few people sitting in the courtroom and took his seat on the left.

All of the spectators were very attentive, but careful not to show any outward sign of emotion. Instead, they wisely chose to pay deference to courtroom decorum. Those who spoke did so in soft, inaudible tones.

A few moments later, attorney D. Webster Stewart, who had been appointed to defend the accused entered from the rear door. He ambled up to the defense table taking his seat across from Harmon Drew. Looking much older than his 60 years, he slid down into the chair, making a point of carefully setting his pen on top of his folder and sliding the water pitcher in front of him to its appropriate spot on the table.

The courtroom was so quiet that you could hear a pin drop. All eyes were on the side door waiting for the judge to appear and start the proceedings. When the side door opened, all eyes were glued to the bailiff who stood near the door and faced the crowd.

"The Honorable Judge John Sandlin, presiding. All rise!" Everyone rose to his or her feet as Judge Sandlin finally entered and took his seat behind the bench.

"This Court is now in session," he banged his gavel. Everyone sat down, anxiously waiting to get a glimpse of the prisoners. Finally, the moment that they were waiting for arrived. Two guards entered in front of the four prisoners. Chester, Mark, Larkin, and Anderson, somberly entered the courtroom with two additional guards bringing up the rear. They cast their eyes down as they entered, fixing them on the floor and took their places near their attorney. Their drab clothing and weary movements bore witness to weeks of sitting in cold drab jail cells, waiting and wondering what the next day would bring. Adversus and Leonard thought that they seemed down-trodden with broken spirits.

The reporters in the room strained to get a good look at each of them, determined to give the best description for their respective newspapers. They looked into the eyes and over the clothes and demeanor of each defendant and chose the most descriptive words that they could muster up.

"Brutish looking." was the depiction that came to mind as a reporter looked at Mark Peters. "with kinky, matted, hair!" he added after pausing slightly.

"Ordinary country Negro." another reporter wrote after glancing at Anderson. "Most likely dim-witted" he added.

It was Larkin's turn to get the once over. "Protruding chin. Appears to be intelligent. Rents in his shoe." was the description that he received.

A reporter described Chester as an "Obvious ringleader." he jotted down. "Imposing presence."

Leonard's eyes were also on Chester. He thought that Chester looked thin and scared. "Of course he is scared!" Leonard thought. "Who wouldn't be under these conditions?"

The judge turned his attention to the four prisoners sitting before him.

"Mark Peters, Chester Tyson, Anderson Heard, and Larkin Stewart, would you please stand."

The judge read the indictments against them.

"You are charged with the murder of Maud Reeves, on the morning of December 25, 1916. "How do you plead?"

One by one, they were arraigned as Judge Sandlin asked each one
 identical questions. At the end of each inquisition, the answer was the same, although the tone in each voice varied.

"Not Guilty! Your Honor..." answered Mark.

"Not! Guilty...your Honor." retorted Larkin.

"not guilty? your honor?" asked Andy in a small voice.

"Not! Guilty! Your! Honor!" Chester stated, emphasizing each word.

That done, jury selection began. Leonard and Adversus anxiously looked on as each of the attorneys questioned the prospective jurors. The law called for a "jury of your peers". Exactly who would the prisonor's "peers" be?

He received his answer very quickly. Their "peers" were twelve white men, most of whom lived nearby.

There were eight farmers on the jury: E.M. Burton, Yellowstone; Sid Harris, Sibley; E.J. Heflin, (of Heflin); A.T. Lee of Leeton; G.L. Herron, Doyline; D.G. Kirkpatrick, Shongoloo; and E.A. Woods, McIntire. One of the farmers, H.G. Griffin, from Heflin, testified that he was 57-years-old "but had never read a newspaper." A merchant from Sibley, Henry Tillman emphatically stated that he "could judge anyone, black or white fairly." The balance of the jury consisted of E.S. Davis, a grocer from Heflin; H.F. Barrington, a patent medicine man from Minden, and John L. Slack, a clerk from Shongoloo. John Slack was selected as jury foreman. All were married men. All denied either hearing about the crime of the century that had taken place in their back yard, or swore that they would not be affected by what they might have heard. All passed muster with few challenges and within the hour, the jury was seated. Harmon Drew glanced at his watch. "Not bad." He thought to himself. "We should be finished by suppertime."

Harmon Drew presented the arguments for the prosecution, carefully laying out the evidence for the jury. He repeatedly referred to the four defendants as "animals" and "degenerates" while describing the viciousness of the crime.

D. Webster Stewart, attorney for the defense followed, seemingly ignoring the case against Chester and Mark. His focus was on the arrest and indictment of Anderson Heard.

"Anderson Heard is a poor, dim-witted negro." he said. "He does not possess the intelligence necessary to formulate a coherent thought. And, furthermore, "Anderson Heard wasn't even at the scene of the crime!"

Jewell Johnson, a neighbor of John Reeves was the first witness called. Haltingly, he answered the questions before him telling the jury what he had seen on that awful day.

He testified that it was the most horrendous scene that he had ever witnessed. Johnson, who lived about a quarter of a mile from John Reeves reflected back to the early morning hours of December 25, 1916 when his neighbor, little Cody Reeves, roused him and some of their neighbors out of their homes, in a panic about "some killins" at the Reeves home.

He repeated the events from that awful morning;

"It sounded real bad." Jewell said. "The little boy was a runnin and a hollerin all through the town. Said he tried to raise up one of his brothers, but he was dead. The boy had blood all over him and was sayin that the whole family was killed. I thought a few of us ought to go check it out." He had testified.

Jewell recounted how he, Will Smith, and J.W. Brazelton enlisted a few of their neighbors, and the Ward boys, and hurried up to the Reeves home.

"And what did you see when you arrived at the property?" D.A. Drew asked gently.

"It was a horrible sight." Jewell cried. "I got to the door and I thought that John might be on a drunk and layin' in wait, so I didn't go in right away. I was getting' ready to call out to him when I heard a child groaning inside. That made up my mind. I pushed the door open and then I saw him."

"Did you notice anything unusual about the door before you went in?" the D.A pressed.

"The door handle had blood on it and there was blood all over the frame." Jewell replied.

"And you say you saw 'him' when you opened the door. Can you tell us who it was that you saw?" Drew continued.

"I saw the boy. Cody's older brother. He was lying on a pallet and looked like he'd been hacked up. I stooped down to pick him up, but he was all bloody. He was barely conscious. I asked him who done that to him but he didn't respond."

"You said it was early morning. Was it light in the house?" Drew asked.

"It was pretty dim. The door was partially open and the sun was comin up so I struck a match so I could see."

"Was anyone else in the house?"

"Well, I went into the bedroom that was just off to the right and I saw…." Jewell hesitated as he remembered John Reeves body lying on the bed.

"And was anyone in the bedroom?" Drew pressed.

"It was John Reeves." John was sprawled across the bed and his skull hacked clean in two. His brains were visible and his left hand was lying at an odd angle across his chest. I knew he was dead."

Jewell was clearly distraught as he finished his testimony. He had just relived the worst day of his life. He was mindful of Reeves' family sitting in the courtroom but he was on the stand and he had to tell it exactly the way that he saw it. He felt bad that the details were so graphic.

Jewell had the full attention of everyone in the courtroom. Everyone's eyes were fixed on the witness stand, straining to hear every word.

He took the D.A. through the rest of the events that he had witnessed, telling how he found the oldest boy with a baby on his lap. The baby was trying to squirm away and the boy was trying to hold him. They were both covered in blood. The children were badly hurt, but still alive, so they took them to the Browder's home to wait for the doctor. They would be taken to Charity hospital. They left Mr. Reeves where he was for the coroner. Once the children had been attended to they went back to the Reeves house. More of the neighbors, and the Sheriff had arrived. The focus was then on finding out who was responsible for the killings.

'One final question," Drew asked Jewell.

"Aside from the children and Mr. Reeves, did you see anyone else in the house?"

"No, Sir." Jewell answered. "I thought that it was curious that Mrs. Reeves was not there."

As Jewell stepped down from the stand, Chester stared straight ahead.

His heart was thumping and his mind was racing a mile a minute, but outwardly, he appeared unemotional, though attentive. The other defendants also exhibited calm outside exteriors, although they knew that their lives hung in the balance.

As the prosecution called a parade of witnesses, it seemed to Adversus and Leonard that the defense attorney, was nothing more than a spectator, himself. Rarely did he object to anything. His cross-examinations were very brief of most witnesses and non-existent for others. His usual answer to, "Do you have any questions of this witness?" was "No questions, Your Honor."

He was very casual and undemanding, rarely participating in the proceedings except occasionally to clarify a point about Anderson or Larkin. Chester wondered why he had an attorney at all. He felt that his fate was already sealed and that the Judge would surely sign his death warrant by the end of the day. Chester usually stared straight ahead, occasionally glancing sideways at the jury or the judge.

The trial moved very quickly throughout most of the afternoon. Bloody overalls and a pair of bloody shoes found in Mark Peters' house were entered into evidence and the blood was positively identified by an expert as human blood. Felix Terrell, a friend of the Peter's family, further identified the clothing as the property of Mark Peters. He had spoken with Mark on Christmas morning about going to see a Christmas tree, but the excursion had not taken place because Mark had been arrested.

W.D. Frazier, a deputy, sheriff, and a witness for the prosecution, identified two blue shirts, one tucked inside the other, both stained with blood and found at the home of Larkin Stewart.

Deputy Earl Taylor was called to the stand. According to Earl, the pistol identified as John Reeves was the same one found between the mattresses at Chester Tyson's home.

"The prosecution calls Zack Martin to the stand."

Chester winced as his father's ax was removed from the plastic bag and paraded before the jury. Dried blood and matted hair were visible on the head of the ax. Chester avoided the jury's eyes. He stared straight ahead.

"Have you ever seen anyone use this particular ax?" Drew asked Zack Martin who was now sitting in the witness box.

"Yes, sir I have."

"And who was that person?"

"John Tyson, Chester Tyson's father."

Will Hawkins was the next person called to the stand. Once again holding the ax, Harmon Drew was questioned about the ax.

"The ax belongs to Chester Tyson," Hawkins began. "but I used it myself just last December to chop wood for Mrs. Tyson, Chester's mother."

"Did you have occasion to speak with Mr. Tyson at that time?"

"No Sir." Will answered. "Chester works up at the mill and he don't stay around much." He answered, avoiding Chester's eyes.

Anderson's brother, Adversus Heard was the next witness to take the stand. Harmon Drew began with the usual questions about how he knew the defendants, where he lived and where he was on the morning of December 25, 1916.

Defense attorney Stewart had said very little throughout the day. He just let the witnesses go on with their stories, rarely objecting even when Chester himself noticed a misstatement or misdirected question. He seemed content to just sit and observe, much like the spectators behind him. Therefore, Chester was startled when Stewart jumped to his feet a few moments later while Adversus was on the stand.

"Anderson Heard arrived early in the morning the day of the murders, is that correct?" Harmon Drew had asked.

"Objection your honor!" Stewart bellowed! "Such timeline has not been established!"

"Sustained!" answered Judge Sandlin.

Moments later, when Judge Sandlin asked Stewart "Do you have any questions for this witness?" D. Webster Stewart jumped to his feet."

"I certainly do, your honor!" he replied.

"You stated that Anderson Heard said that he was at the Reeves home on the day of the murders, is that correct?" he asked.

"Yes Sir, that's right." Adversus said.

"And exactly what time of day was it when you encountered Anderson Heard?" he continued.

"It was about eight o'clock in the morning. It was after breakfast and Anderson said he had just went up to the house and seen a terrible sight." Adversus replied.

"So, are you saying that it was *after* eight o'clock in the morning when you encountered him?"

"Yes, suh."

"And did he say whether he saw the murders take place?"

"No, Suh. He say he wasn't there when it happen."

"Did he say where he was the night before?'

"Yes, suh." He say he was sleepin ova to Chester's house 'cause he wanted to go to Chester's wedding."

"And at no time did he say that he was anywhere near the Reeves home earlier that morning?"

"That's right, suh. He say when he got there, the place was filled up with the police and sech." Adversus finished.

"I have no further questions of this witness, you honor." Webster Stewart said triumphantly. He had driven home the point that Anderson was not present at the time of the murders. Seeming to bow before the jury, he sat back down in his chair and quickly jotted something down on the tablet.

Chester was glad that at least Stewart had proven one point. Anderson should not be tried. He was nowhere near the place that night.

Chester took a deep breath wondering when Johnny would arrive. Johnny was his ace in the hole. Chester had been surprised that Johnny had already come through for them in a big way when he told the sheriff that Henry Waller had committed the crime. He'd heard about Johnny's confession. He knew that Johnny had told all of it. The sheriff knew that Waller had forced them to go against their will. He knew that Waller was the one that used the ax to commit the murders. And soon the court would know the truth.

It was very late in the afternoon when the Prosecution called the next witness.

"The State would like to call Will Loyd to the stand." Harmon Drew announced.

Slowly, but deliberately a tall colored man made his way to the stand. Something about the way he walked seemed familiar to Chester. However, the name did not sound familiar. Curiously, he looked at the man, as Will Loyd sat down in the witness stand.

"Please state your name for the court."

"Will Loyd." he answered.

"And Mr. Loyd, can you tell the court where you are employed?"

Still curious, Chester was trying to figure out why Will's voice sounded so familiar. Moments later, he got his answer.

"I am currently employed by the Price Detective Agency as a private detective." Will stated.

It was all Chester could do to keep from reacting. He knew this person as "Ellis". It was his old cellmate from the jail in Texarkana! Suddenly Chester felt angered and betrayed.

"How long have you worked for the Price Brother's detective agency?" Harmon Drew asked, gathering information on Will Loyd's background.

"Off and on for bout two years."

"Price Brother's detective agency?" Chester pondered. "Two years??" Mr. Price had questioned Chester personally, and Chester did not say two words to him. So he decided to sic "Ellis" on him?

Harmon Drew continued to question the witness. "And during your employment, did you have an assignment at the Texarkana correctional facility in January of this year?

"Yes sir," Will said. "I was assigned to gather information from a suspect who was held there.

"And why was a private detective needed gather information from this particular suspect."

"The suspect had refused to talk to any of the other detectives. Detective Price thought that I might be able to gain his trust, and get him to talk to me." Will said.

"And do you see that person in this courtroom today?" Harmon Drew continued.

"Yes, Sir. I do."

"And can you identify that suspect for the court?"

"Yes, Sir. It's the defendant sitting on the right side of Mr. Stewart. Chester Tyson." he answered.

Will Loyd recounted the days he had spent in the cell with Chester. He stayed in the cell for two days so that he could slowly build Chester's trust. He mislead Chester and pretended to know nothing about the case. Will told the court that he lied and told Chester that he had robbed a bank and killed two deputy sheriffs. He said he lied about his family. He lied about having children. He lied about his name. He lied about his criminal background, and finally Chester talked about the murders.

"Did Chester tell you his whereabouts in the early morning hours of Christmas Day?

"Yes Sir. He said he was at the Reeves' house."

"And what was he doing at the Reeves' house?" Attorney Drew questioned.

"He said he was standing guard outside of the home while the murders were committed." Will stated.

At that point, Chester looked directly at Will Loyd, but Will was staring straight ahead.

"And to think I trusted that nigger!" Chester thought. "And here he done sold me out!" He was furious. Nevertheless, he managed to maintain a calm outward demeanor.

"Did Chester Tyson say whether or not he brought any sort of weapon to the Reeves' house?" was the next question.

"Yes Sir, he said he brought an ax.....he said he was forced to bring his ax."

Chester waited for the rest to come out. All of it. He had told "Ellis" about Henry Waller. He had explained how Waller forced him to go. Now would be a good time for his attorney to cross-examine Will Loyd and get the truth out about who really committed the murders.

However, Harmon Drew never specifically asked about Henry Waller or any whites being involved. And Will Loyd never offered the information. The opportunity was lost.

"No further questions of this witness, your Honor." he finished.

After Will left the witness box, a parade of officers and deputies appeared in quick succession to tell what they had heard and seen in the days following the murders.

Upon questioning, Sheriff Phillips vehemently denied that he had intimidated or abused "the negroes" into confessing. "They freely con-fessed." He testified.

"Peters readily admitted that he was there, almost immediately." said one officer after he was asked about the confessions.

"Larkin Stewart did not admit that he was there." said another. "At least not when he was first questioned."

"Anderson Heard did not make a formal statement to the Webster Parish Sheriff." further testimony revealed.

"Chester Tyson admitted he was there, but the first time he made a statement was just last night." Offered Deputy Bazer.

"No, he did not admit to committing the crime." he answered to a follow up question.

More witnesses were called to answer questions about the crime scene. Jewell Johnson was recalled.

"And was Mrs. Reeves ever located?"

"Yes, sir." said Jewell Johnson.

"And can you tell us about her appearance when you first saw her?"

"She was lying face down near the rear of the house and appeared to have been hacked with a hatchet or an ax. She also had what appeared to be a gunshot wound to the temple." stated Jewell.

"And what lead you to the homes of Mark Peters and Chester Tyson?"

"There were three tracks of blood that led away from the Waller house. We followed those tracks, and the dogs picked up the scent."

The parade of witnesses continued to come and go very rapidly with little input from Webster Stewart. Therefore, Chester was astonished when once again Stewart rose to his feet after the judge's next question.

"Would the defense like to cross examine this witness?'

"Yes, I would, your Honor!" Stewart declared.

He took a couple of steps towards the witness.

"You said that the tracks of blood led you directly to the homes of Chester Tyson and Mark Peters?" he questioned Sheriff Phillips. "Is that correct?"

"Yes, sir, that is correct." Sheriff Phillips answered.

"And once more for clarification, can you tell the court exactly how many tracks of blood were visible."

"Three sets."

"Can you repeat that please?" He asked, turning his back on the witness and facing the jury.

"There were three tracks of blood."

"Just three? Are you certain? Not four?"

"Yes sir. There were just three tracks."

"I have no further questions for this witness." Stewart finished.

Stewart made his way back to his seat, apparently satisfied that he had driven home the point that there were only three tracks of blood, and four men standing accused. Surely, it would be apparent that Anderson Heard wasn't even there.

Apparently, Harmon Drew was not willing to concede this point.

"Re-direct?" the Judge asked.

"Yes, your Honor." answered Drew.

"Sheriff Phillips, you said that there were only three tracks of blood leading away from the Reeves home, is that correct?"

"That's correct."

"Considering the amount of blood that was found about the property, would it have been possible for more than three individuals to have been at the property at the time of the crime, yet only have three sets of footprints found?"

"It's very possible." answered Phillips.

"How so?"

"Well, there are a number of ways a person could leave without leaving any shoe tracks. They could have removed their shoes. They might have taken another route. They could have left by horse. Or they could have left in an automobile.

"No further questions, your Honor."

Finally the prosecution rested. All of the evidence had been presented. They were confident that they had proven their case.

CHAPTER 8

THE VERDICT

Chester stretched his legs during the much-needed break, reflecting on the day. Many of the revelations in court had taken him by surprise. Much of the testimony threw him. His attorney had discussed little with him aside from telling him to keep his mouth shut and not show any outbursts. Mr. Stewart had gathered their statements from them and made a few notes, but there was no real defense strategy that he knew of. He felt that he had already been tried and convicted.

Court reconvened at seven o'clock that evening. Few people had left the courtroom and every seat was filled. After everyone had taken their seats, the Judge entered and everyone rose as dictated by courtroom etiquette, and then returned to their seats. It was time for the defense to present its case. Chester did not have a clue as to which witnesses would be called, but he expected that Johnny Long would surely be the star witness. Johnny was white. And that carried a lot of weight.

Stewart called exactly two witnesses. Both of them had already testified for the prosecution. Webster Stewart attempted to show that there was no proof that Larkin Stewart and Anderson Heard were in any way connected to the crimes. No physical evidence had been positively linked to them. "In fact," he stated, "the only thing that all of the other witnesses agreed on was that Anderson Heard was not there!"

"Are there any more witnesses for the defense?" Judge Sandlin finally asked.

"No your honor. However, at this time each of the defendants would like to make voluntary statements to the court."

Chester, Mark, Larkin, and Anderson all jerked their heads around and stared at him. "What did he say?" they thought.

"Objection your honor! Objection!" Harmon Drew jumped to his feet.

"The State objects to this tactic due to the fact that 'voluntary statements' are not sworn statements, and cannot be cross-examined in open court. I would submit that these 'voluntary statements' are in fact testimony that is subject to cross-examination. This is nothing more than an attempt by the defense to by-pass the right of the people to cross-examine these witnesses."

"Please approach the bench." the Judge ordered.

"As Judge Sandlin, Harmon Drew and Webster Stewart discussed the proceedings at the bench, Chester's mind began to wander. Johnny Long had not been called as a witness. In fact, the name "Henry Waller" as the one who swung the ax was never mentioned at all. There had been a few times when one of the deputies started to mention the statements that the negro defendants or Johnny Long had made, implicating Henry Waller, but they were quickly shut down. The jury had heard enough to know that the two white men were involved, but they were instructed to disregard most of the statements regarding them.

Soon both attorneys returned to their seats. Stewart turned to his four clients and gave them their instructions. "You just go up there and tell the same thing that you told me yesterday. No more. No less. You understand?" he instructed.

Anderson Heard was the first one to take the stand.

"I ain't seen no killin's and I ain't been at that house on Christmas Eve. I only told dat deputy dat I was there cuz he knocked me around and said he'd let em lynch me if I didn't confess. It was real bad up to that jailhouse and I was scared. So I lied about being there because he tol' me it would be worse for me if I kept denying it. I swear, your Honor, that I am telling the truth now. I was at my cousin Chester's house, and I fell asleep on the sofa early dat night!"

Larkin Stewart was the next one to make his statement. He told a similar story to Anderson's, saying that he had confessed but that he was forced into the confession. He denied being at the scene of the crime and denied any knowledge of the murders until the following day. He said that Mark Peters was either confused or not telling the truth when Mark said Larkin was at the Waller house on the night of the murders.

Mark Peters took the witness stand. He didn't look intimidated. In fact, he looked angry. Even though Stewart had told them not to add anything to their stories, Mark added a very important fact. Although he had been questioned hundreds of times about the murders he always stopped short of invoking the name of the "white man" who wielded the ax. This time, Mark was more forthcoming.

"Henry Waller came to my house and forced us to go." Mark flatly stated. "We didn't want to. But we knew that he would kill us if we didn't. So me, Chester, and Larkin went over there. That white kid, Johnny Long was with us too."

The jury was intently listening to his testimony, as was the rest of the crowd in the courtroom.

"It was Henry." he said finally. "Henry killed all of them people with that ax. He said he would kill us all if we told, even if it took him forty years to do it."

You could hear a pin drop. The members of the jury had leaned forward in their seats, many of them cocking an ear to the side to make sure that they did not miss a word. Others fervently took notes on the pads lying before them.

Chester was the last of the defendants called to make his statement.

He took the stand, and looked out over the crowd. "Hostile" was the word that came to his mind as he looked at the spectators. He decided to focus on the few friendly black faces that were in the rear. Wanting to make sure that his family knew that he was not a monster, he began his story. It was the first time that he had told all of it. Sure, he had told parts of it to Will Loyd when he thought that Will was "Ellis" in the Texarkana jail. And he had told part of it to Sheriff Hughes last night. However, it seemed like Sheriff Hughes didn't want to know the truth. He was badgering Chester and giving him the third degree when Chester finally admitted that he knew who swung the ax and killed the Reeves'. And Chester said that it wasn't him.

Sheriff Hughes, angry and frustrated that Chester would blame Henry Waller, had warned Chester many times against implicating an innocent white man.

"You are asking for trouble, boy." he had said.

Like Mark, Chester had never mentioned Henry Waller by name when questioned by Hughes. When he got the part about the actual swinging of the ax and the identity of the ax-man, he clammed up. However, today would be different. He had nothing to lose. If the expressions in the eyes the crowd was any indication, he was already a dead man. So when he spoke, it was because he didn't want his family to think that he was a murderer. He started with the eleven o'clock hour when he opened the door that night to find Henry Waller standing there. Henry stood with his shotgun in hand and was drunk as a skunk.

"I didn't want to go. It was Christmas Eve, and I was supposed to get married the next day, and I just wanted to go to bed. But Henry Waller roused me up and made me get my ax."

"We walked ova to Mark's house and Johnny and Larkin was there." he continued.

116

"Johnny was actin real strange, and Mr. Waller kepta tellin us that we was just going to play some cards and drink some whiskey. I didn't want to go, but I figured that I could get out of it after a spell."

"When we gets to the house, it was dark and quiet and I said we should leave." he stated emphatically.

"Waller tol' me to call 'im out" Chester said. "I said again that we should leave 'cause they was probably sleep, but Mr. Waller jest kept on pushin. I just stood there and finally Mr. Waller and Johnny went into the house."

Chester took a deep breath. Maybe he should stop before he said too much. If he told what happened next, the courtroom might erupt into a brawl. He might be taken out and lynched before the day was out for implicating someone that many considered an upstanding white citizen in the community. But even if he died today, he wanted his mother to know that her son was innocent. So he took a deep breath and continued.

"Right after they went in the house I heard a bunch of crashes and noises and I heard a baby cryin. Mrs. Reeves run out uh the house and Mr. Waller was uh chasin' her. He chased her 'round back and I heard him hit her with the ax, and I heard a shotgun go off. Waller come back around and went back in the house." Chester paused to clarify in his mind what had taken place next. "I heard something sliding across the floor and something soundin' like somebidy hammerin' open a metal box – kinda like hinges breakin'. Next thang I knowed, Waller come out and washed his hands in a bucket of wata by the porch and calls us all ova there. I thought he was gonna kill us too, but he give me the pistol and the ax and tol me to get rid of 'em. He changed his socks and give Mark his shoes back. Then he tol' us that he would kill us all if any of us said a word about what happen. Him and Johnny went one way and we went the other way. I swear, your Honor, that I didn't know that anyone was gonna be killed that night" he concluded directing his last statement directly to the Judge.

After Chester's statement, the prosecution again pressed for the right to cross-examine the suspects.

"The defense has used the term "voluntary statements" for the accused, as nothing more than a tactic to prevent the State from its right to cross-examination" Harmon Drew objected. "The State demands the right to cross examine these witnesses."

After a second denial from Judge Sandlin, Harmon Drew began his closing arguments.

"The prosecution has proven its case." he addressed the jury.

"Even though you have heard statements from the defendants," the DA continued, "those statements cannot be deemed as reliable because they were not subject to cross examination and review by the State. You have before you, conclusive evidence that proves that all four of these defendants played a crucial role in the murders of the Reeves Family. The ax belonged to Chester Tyson and the tracks of blood led directly to Chester and Mark. The pistol belonging to Mr. Reeves was found in Chester Tyson's own bed. And the clothing that they wore that night was found in their homes, still warm with the blood of the victims." He paused to let the evidence take full effect on the jury."

"Therefore, The People of the State of Louisiana ask, that you return a verdict of "Guilty as Charged With Capital Punishment" for Larkin Stewart, Mark Peters and Chester Tyson. We also ask," he concluded. "That at a minimum, you return a verdict of 'guilty without capital punishment' against Anderson Heard." With that, he took his seat.

Webster Stewart's closing statements were brief and generally dispassionate. He did not rehash the statements about Henry Waller being the instigator of the crime. He barely touched on anyone else being involved.

He briefly reviewed the highlights of the testimony and pointed out a few of the defects:

"Remember, gentlemen, that there were only three tracks of blood at the crime scene. And you have before you four Negroes accused of murder. You learned that Anderson Heard is a "dim-witted negro" who lacks the capacity to formulate a coherent account of the facts. The statements that he made in the Webster Parish jail cannot be relied upon because he simply wanted to impress the police officers by telling them what he thought would please them."

"No evidence," he reiterated. "was found that connects Anderson Heard or Larkin Stewart to the crime."

"Therefore," he concluded. "the defense asks that you spare the lives of Mark Peters and Chester Tyson. We further ask that you return a verdict of 'not guilty' against Larkin Stewart and Anderson Heard.

With that, he took his seat. Testimony had concluded. The case was handed to the jury at 12:30 am on January 30, 1917. Everyone expected a speedy verdict. Most had been there all day. "Just one more hour" many reasoned, "and the jury will come back. The judge is gonna hang 'em all" they predicted. They were looking forward to being there when that sentence was pronounced! They would get to hear the judge sentence four men to die!

Chester's family was hopeful, yet doubtful. They had seen nothing within the proceedings that led them to believe that the outcome would be anything except a guilty verdict.

"Even their attorney" they reasoned, "only asked that they not hang."

Many of them were surprised that the case had come to trial at all, with all the threats of lynching that they had heard about since the murders. It wasn't something that most whites admitted to, when outsiders asked about racism in Louisiana.

"We are a peaceful community." they would say. "Everyone gets along jest fine. It's all you outsiders who are always trying to start somethin' up."

They were very protective of their image. Many black folks and white folks were outwardly cordial to one another. They nodded "hello" in passing or occasionally stopped to talk. But most of the colored residents lived on one side of town and the white residents lived on the other. There was a general mistrust of each other. There was very little socializing. The very fact that Chester and the others had occasionally played cards together was somewhat of an anomaly. In fact, it was against the law for blacks and whites to socialize in most drinking establishments. Some ignored the law, but it was on the books. There was suspicion on both sides.

It was no different on that day in the courtroom. People stayed in their comfort zone as they discussed the trial. There were small groups of white men. There were small groups of black men. And there were small groups of women.

Several of the spectators attempted to gain the attention of the District Attorney or the accused. An occasional question, directed at one of the accused men could be heard.

"Which one of you boys really swung that ax?"

"Do you think you will get the death penalty?'

"Why didn't you get rid of the pistol?"

A few people had gained Larkin Stewarts attention and once again, he denied any knowledge of the murders. The press was eager to take photographs of the prisoners and flashbulbs occasionally popped in their direction. But because of the little swinging door between the spectators and the prisoners, most could not get close enough to get a clear photograph.

Sheriff Phillips watched the attempts to get a glimpse of the prisoners. A reporter noticed the Sheriff and yelled. "Can you bring 'em closer for a picture Sheriff?" Feeling like somewhat of a celebrity, Sheriff Phillips was very accommodating to the press. He walked over to the prisoners and pushed them towards the crowd.

"Stand over here, boys!" he directed.

Following his directions, the four of them moved towards the crowd. As if he were introducing a theatre ensemble, he pointed to each one and called them by name.

"This here is Mark Peters. Next to Mark is Larkin Stewart. That one there is Chester Tyson, and down on the end is Anderson Heard."

"Can you have 'em stand closer together so we can get a better picture of 'em."

Sheriff Phillips motioned for the prisoners to scoot closer together. They silently complied and somberly faced the crowd. Pleased with the outcome, bright flash-bulbs and rapid clicks from the camera's popped and snapped as the moment was captured by the members of the press. Those who were lucky enough have a camera ready and close enough to get a good shot were elated!

Lively chatter filled the courtroom when about an hour later the door to the deliberation room opened. Everyone rushed to his or her seat, excitedly anticipating the verdict.

But the verdict had not been reached. The bailiff was just forwarding questions that the jury had for the judge. The judge took his seat and attorneys Stewart and District attorney Harmon Drew returned. The bailiff stood on the side of the podium while the judge reviewed the papers on his desk. The judge then turned to the bailiff.

"Please bring in the jury." he stated.

The jury took their seats and the judge directed his questions to foreman.

"Okay, you say that you are unable to reach a verdict, Mr. Slack?"

"Yes, sir. We can't come to an agreement."

"Just how divided are you?" Judge Sandlin inquired.

"Well, Sir. We are pretty much divided all around. Eight are leaning to manslaughter or guilty without capital punishment against all four Negroes. And you got four holdin' out for guilty as charged with the hanging."

"Well, I know that you have heard an abundance of testimony today. If I give you some more time do you think that you can reach a verdict this evening?"

"Well, your Honor. To be honest with you, we are really confused about this whole thing. Truth is, we're wondering if we return a verdict of guilty as charged against the negroes if there can still be a trial to get Henry Waller convicted too? We are all pretty much in agreement that Waller is the principle figure in this thing. We 're not sure what verdicts we can return against the negroes and still preserve a case against the other fellow."

Clearly startled, Judge Sandlin sat straight up in his seat! He cringed, aware of the fact that all the members of the press were excitedly taking notes. His face reddened as he imagined what the next headline of the day would be:

"White man found guilty at Negro Trial!"

"Mistrial – Stupid Judge Questions Jurors in open Court"

"Judge Sandlin Embarrassed at Error"

He quickly began speaking before Mr. Slack could say anything further.

"Mr. Slack, the only individuals on trial today are those listed in the indictments that you hold. Any evidence against any other person bears no weight on the verdicts that are to be returned against those on trial in this court today." he took a deep breath, hoping that Mr. Slack had noticed his stern tone.

"As per your instructions, you have four verdicts that you might return." He continued. "Those verdicts are as follows. One: Guilty as Charged, which carries with it a mandate for capital punishment. Two: Guilty without Capital Punishment. Three: Guilty of Manslaughter, or Four: Acquittal. Do you understand those verdicts?"

"Yes, Sir."

"Those verdicts," Judge Sandlin continued, "Can apply to any of the accused individually, or be given to all of the individuals collectively. Each and every individual is entitled a verdict based solely on the evidence presented against him. Does that help you?"

"Yes, Sir. Thank you, Sir." Mr. Slack said before returning to the jury room.

Judge Sandlin then turned his attention to the courtroom.

"This jury will be sequestered for the rest of the evening, and these proceedings will resume at 8:30 a.m." he announced banging his gavel on the wooden block. He then rose and walked over to the bailiff. He instructed him to sequester the jury until the following morning and have them return rested and ready for final deliberations.

At 8:00 the following morning the crowd outside of the courtroom was even larger than it had been the day before. Word had spread that the case was in the hands of the jury. People wanted to be in the courtroom when the jury returned. Once again, every seat in the courtroom was filled with spectators and there was a large overflow crowd outside of it. Some of the press in attendance had come all the way from California.

This time their wait was not long. Refreshed and apparently clearer than they were the night before, the jury sent word at 9:30 am that they had reached a verdict.

All eyes were on the jury as the bailiff led them in. They avoided looking out into the crowd, and their eyes were void of any hint of their findings. Judge Sandlin glanced over the verdicts and nodded to the jury, indicating that everything was in place.

Turning his eyes to the accused, he said, "Anderson Heard and Larkin Stewart, will you please stand?"

Along with their attorney, they rose to their feet, their calm exterior contradicted by their shaking knees and the lumps in their throats. The jury had decided their fate!

"Anderson Heard and Larkin Stewart," he began. "...by reason of the law, and of the evidence being in favor of the state, and by further reason of a bill of indictment charging you, the defendants with murder, I hereby deliver these verdicts."

The jury finds that you are guilty as charged, without capital punishment. It is ordered, adjudged and decreed as defendants for the said crime, you shall be confined at hard labor in the Louisiana State Prison for a period of your natural lives... You may be seated."

"Mark Peters and Chester Tyson, will you please stand?" He said turning his attention to the other two defendants.

The two of them rose slowly. They appeared to be calm and detached. But their rapidly beating hearts belied their composed exterior. Certain that they already knew what the verdict would be, they stood and faced Judge Sandlin. Judge Sandlin read the verdict:

"In this cause, and by reason of the law, the jury finds the evidence being in favor of the State and against you, the accused. And by further reason of the indictments and endorsements thereon; The verdict of the jury finds you the accused, GUILTY of MURDER as charged. Further, it is ordered, adjudged and decreed that you, Mark Peters, and you, Chester Tyson be HANGED BY THE NECK UNTIL YOU ARE DEAD.

It is so ordered, that the officer designated by law will execute this judgment according to law at a time and upon a day to be fixed by the Governor of the State of Louisiana."

Chester fought down the urge to reach for the chair behind him. He wasn't clear on much of what the judge had said, but he did hear "GUILTY", as well as, "HANGED BY THE NECK UNTIL YOU ARE DEAD." He stared straight ahead refusing to react. He appeared stoic and resigned. Mark stood transfixed and sturdy. He did not bat an eye.

The judge banged his gavel on the block, rose, and quickly exited the courtroom

The spectators in the courtroom finally released their pent-up emotions. They shouted their proclamations of agreement, and in a manner befitting a final curtain call of a grand theatrical production, they clapped wildly and gleefully, stating their general approval. The trial, as expected had been a sensational one. There would be a hanging as vindication for the lives of an innocent family. They were jubilant at the outcome.

But there was no joy in Mariah's eyes. She had attended the sentencing, seated in the rear and surrounded by family. Whereas others in the courtroom perceived Chester and the others to be calm and unaffected by the verdicts, she had looked into their eyes. In Chester's eyes, she saw panic. She had seen a glimmer of hope in his eyes at the beginning of the trial. The hope slowly gave way to resignation, and at the pronouncement of the sentence, his eyes had darkened with horror and fear. She knew her son. His eyes revealed what was in his heart and his mind. And he felt like death waited just outside his window.

Mariah could also see the anger in Mark's eyes. There wasn't a bit of surprise though, she thought. It was as if he had expected it all along. When Mark had made his voluntary statements to the court, he appeared resigned to his fate. However, hearing the judge sentence him to a hanging undoubtedly caused a deep sense of rage that his eyes could not conceal.

Although he was not as enraged as Mark, Larkin's eyes reflected both sadness and confirmation that his expectations had been met. If anything, he had been slightly surprised that the jury had decided against slipping his head into a noose. The only one who seemed to be completely taken aback by his sentence was Anderson Heard. Mariah witnessed the deep breaths that her nephew took. There was a terrified and confused look about his eyes. He barely maintained his composure, and was unprepared for the guilty verdict.

Mariah's tears fell as she hung her head in grief. Her son had just been handed a death sentence. And the reactions of those around her were jovial and exuberant!

"Look at them!" someone was saying about the new convicts. "They don't even care! I'm glad that they got what they deserved!"

"The sooner they hang, the better!" said another. "Animals!"

The crowd was still milling about outside when the four prisoners were brought out of the courtroom, sandwiched between Sheriff Phillips, Deputy Sheriff Milam Miller, and Detective T.D. Price. They marched them to the Webster Parish jail, followed closely by many of the members of the crowd, who were determined to stay close to them as to not miss anything. Some were still there hours later when the prisoners left for the Caddo jail for processing. They boarded the LR & N train late that evening for the long trip to the Penitentiary in Baton Rouge.

Back in the safety of their own homes, Mariah, and her sister Georgia discussed the day's events with some of the other family members. Feeling hurt and angry, they now could say what they had wanted to scream in court.

"Fair trial, my foot!" Mariah cried. "Did you see 'em? All them white people!? They were more interested in getting home to dinner than convicting an innocent nigger to hang! I told you! The whole trial was a game to them! Wouldn't of even been no trial if those reporters weren't stayin' on it! They would have hung 'em dat very night if nobody was a watchin' em. Only difference is now they can say it's a legal hangin."

"That for sho!" Georgia said. "Andy ain't had no cause to be in that jail et all! Twern't even there!" she declared. "Everybidy know'd good and well 'twas that white man who did them killins! He got off Scott free cuz dey done found somebidy to hang in his place." she said defiantly. Any ol' nigger'll do to take a hanging for a white man. Always did! Always will."

As they spoke, thoughts about their many trials and tribulations over the years filled their heads. They had both been through slavery. They were in their twenties when they watched black men in the south hold important political offices. They were in their thirties when they saw many of the black men who had been voted into political offices lynched, tricked or intimidated into returning the power to the white class.

The following years proved to be tumultuous as Jim Crow was solidified and they were viewed as second-class citizens. Mariah saw little difference in slavery and freedom.

"You got four colored men on trial." Mariah stated. "And it takes jest one day to call a jury, have a trial, and order a hanging! Has that ever happened to a white man?!"

They knew that it hadn't. At least not as far as they could see. But in the end, they knew that it was useless to argue. Injustice was always swift.

The Shreveport Times Article Jan 31, 1917

Courtesy of Shreve Memorial Library

Chester Tyson's WWI Draft Registration Card

States "*In Jail, Convicted of Murder, Waiting to be Hung*"

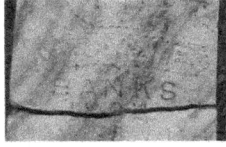

Mealy Banks Headstone in Newsome Cemetery

Reads *"Melie Banks 1804-1919 Age 115"*

The Home of John Nelson Reeves

Courtesy of State Library of Louisiana (http://www.state.lib.la.us)

CHAPTER 9

Henry Waller on Trial

It was nearly midnight when Chester, Mark, Larkin and Anderson arrived at the Penitentiary. The guards stripped them of their dignity and assigned them a prison number. They were issued their prison gear, which consisted of black and white striped prison shirts and pants, a blanket, regulation shoes and underwear. Heavy chains on their ankles were part of the package. They were taken to their cells, which were nothing more than cold dank cubicles surrounded by heavy black iron bars and bare concrete walls. The cots, if you were lucky enough to get one, were thin and lay on cold concrete slabs.

In the night, screaming, fighting, and unimaginable cries of pain were heard coming from the other prisoners. Tomorrow they would begin their first day of hard labor in the Penitentiary. Chester knew of others who had been sentenced to Louisiana State Prison. It was known as the most horrific prison in the south. Many died there – some at the hands of other prisoners or prison officials. Others died from neglect or broken hearts. Some people called the Penitentiary "Angola" which was the name of the town in which it was situated. Others simply called it the "the Farm," because it was an actual Prison Farm where the inmates harvested vegetable crops, and raised cattle. These items were sold on the open market.

In fact, the *Farm* had once been an actual slave plantation. Some of Chester's own relatives were likely enslaved there prior to emancipation. Now, he was in a similar situation. During slavery, you were forced to stay, you worked for no pay and could be whipped at the whim of the slave owner. In prison, you were on lockdown, worked for no pay and you could be beaten at the whim of the prison guards. Chester saw no difference between the two. And while he sat in prison, Henry Waller was yet to be tried.

Earlier that day in Webster Parish, the grand jury had completed their work against the two white men. Just as Chester and Mark had received their sentence to hang, the grand jury had indicted Henry Waller and Johnny Long for the very same crime –the murder of Mrs. Maude Reeves. The Waller trial would take place on March 12, 1917, which was about six weeks later. The trial would be very different from the "Negro" trial. Henry Waller would have the very best attorneys in the Parish. The district attorney would carefully prepare and make sure that all of his "t's" were crossed and his "i's were dotted. Everyone would follow the law to the letter to avoid any accusations of impropriety. Every precaution would be taken. The prosecution would tread carefully, knowing that the defense would vehemently object to improper questions.

Henry Waller's family was well respected in the community. They had the resources to mount a proper defense. And above all, Henry Waller was white. Johnny's trial would be held separately to insure fairness and judicial parity.

Six weeks later, Chester and the others had settled into their difficult routine at Angola Prison. Through the prison grapevine, they had heard that the Waller trial had begun. They thought that Waller would receive a quick "not-guilty" verdict. When no word of a verdict came that evening, they wondered if the charges had been dropped.

However, the trial was still in session. Jury selection had continued from the first day, and testimony had not yet begun. The community met the day of the Waller trial with much anticipation. They had already learned a great deal of information since the Tyson trial and they were curious about Henry Waller. They wanted more information. For some, the second trial brought even more questions than answers. For example, since the negroes had already been convicted, would Henry Waller go free? Did the Negroes and Johnny Long really frame Henry Waller? If Henry were convicted, would Chester and Mark still hang?

Some people had experienced a change of heart after Chester and Mark were sentenced to hang. Many were now convinced that Henry Waller was the real killer and that the four black men convicted of the crime were merely dupes of his grand scheme. They were convinced that there had been a rush to judgment in the arrest and indictments of Chester and the other negroes. Many people now openly questioned their guilt. But the fact remained that innocent children had been killed, and they wanted the right head to swing in the noose. They were there to ensure that that happened.

Others were not so kind. Mariah's family had received numerous notes at their doorstep demanding, "Niggers get out!" She vowed to stand her ground. She thought that eventually the hatred would die down. However, the threats continued almost daily. Some of the neighbors still wanted them to move for their "own protection". Others wanted them to move for the "good of the community". Getting up in the morning to face another day became a huge challenge. Although curious about the Waller trial, they decided to stay away from the courthouse to avoid the press and any racial friction.

The Webster Parish courtroom and the areas around it were overflowing with people from near and far who had come to see Part Two of the trial of the century. Security was just as tight as the first trial. Numerous deputies searched the spectators prior to allowing them into the courtroom, which filled up very quickly. Armed guards enthusiastically policed the area and were on the lookout for any troublemakers or those wishing to do harm to the prisoner.

In contrast to the Negro trial, the wheels of justice moved very slowly for the Waller trial. Although there was only one man on trial, jury selection stalled on the very first day because too many potential jurors had heard about Waller and knew too much about the murders. Many of them admitted that they had formed opinions. The attorneys on both sides took great care to excuse any potential juror that they did not deem amenable to their position. An additional pool of possible jurors had to be summoned, and the selection process continued the following day.

An acceptable jury was finally seated on the second day of the trial. The parade of subpoenaed witnesses faced an aggressive prosecution team and an even more aggressive defense team. The jury would face an aggressive trial. Harmon Drew presented the case for the prosecution, along with the Honorable J.M. Foster of Shreveport.

Thomas W. Robertson acted as attorney for Henry Waller's defense. He was expected to aggressively fight the charges for his client. Finally it was time for opening statements.

"The State will show that not only is Henry Waller a pathological liar, he is also a cold-blooded murderer." Drew began.

"We will present evidence to show beyond any reasonable doubt that Henry Waller took an ax, purposefully and callously killed members of an innocent family and then casually went out and celebrated Christmas day!" he stated passionately, looking at the jury.

"Signed confessions will clearly show that on Christmas Eve, December 24, 1916, Henry Waller attempted to cover his tracks by soliciting a number of unwitting negroes to accompany him for the express purpose of creating an alibi."

"The defense will try to trick you by saying that Henry Waller was too far away to commit this heinous crime. But we will show that not only was it physically possible for Mr. Waller to be in Serepta and then Grove within the early morning hours Christmas day, but that Henry Waller willfully and wantonly, and with malice aforethought, entered the home of the Reeves family. We will show that he viciously took the lives of not only two caring parents, but also of three innocent children. And Gentlemen, after you have viewed all of this evidence, you will have no choice but to reach a verdict of 'Guilty' on all counts."

Not to be outdone, the defense attorney took his place before the jury.

"Gentlemen of the jury," attorney Robertson began slowly. "There are no material facts that would cause any reasonable person to conclude that Mr. Waller is guilty of these charges. There is no weapon and no physical evidence that shows that he was anywhere near the Reeves home on the night of the murders. In fact, we will prove to you that it was a physical impossibiltiy for him to have committed these crimes, and at the end of the day you will find that Mr. Henry Waller is not guilty!"

With that, the prosecution began its carefully laid out case. Laying the foundation, Harmon Drew called Cody Reeves to the stand.

Looking very small in the big witness seat, seven-year-old Cody effectively and bravely recounted the early morning hours of the murders. Describing his fear and his terror, he told of finding his father hacked to death and his brothers battered and bleeding. He told of running as fast as he could to the nearest house to get help. The little boy's testimony elicited the exact effect intended by the prosecution. He was their "sympathy vote." There wasn't a dry eye in the courtroom as Cody described his excitement as he woke up in anticipation of presents on Christmas morning and instead saw his father and brothers covered in blood!

The defense was also very gentle in its questioning of the boy. Neither side wanted to appear unfeeling towards a young child who had witnessed such a horrific sight. Through gentle questioning, the prosecution had managed to paint the picture of the heinous crime that had been committed, and the defense had managed to show that no identification of the person responsible for the crime had been made from Cody's testimony.

Following Cody, a succession of witnesses to the scene of the crime was called. The Brazelton's and Jewell Johnson told about the physical condition of the house and of the horror of finding of the bodies inside of it. Sheriff Phillips described finding Maude Reeves outside of the house, facedown and barefoot with a gaping hole in her head.

Doc Tompkins gave a detailed account of the condition of each body and time-stamped probable time of the death of Mr. and Mrs. Reeves and each child.

Numerous neighbors described the blood and other physical evidence surrounding the home, and the tracks of blood leading both into and away from it.

The defense did not let any piece of evidence go unchallenged. They aggressively countered each point, rigorously questioning Doc Tompkins about his timing of the murders. As to the description of the numerous tracks of blood going into and out of the house, they took that opportunity to show that all of the evidence had been compromised, because neighbors had moved unfettered both inside and outside of the home for hours, therefore contaminating the crime scene before it could be preserved.

Sheriff Phillips and Sheriff Hughes testified to the activities in the days following the crime and the arrests of the suspects. When they mentioned Johnny Long, all eyes and ears were upon them, intently listening. There was great interest in the white suspect who had spoken out against Henry Waller in favor of the negroes. They knew that Johnny was a key witness, and the entire case could turn based on his statements.

The signed confession that Johnny had made to Sheriff Phillips was of utmost importance.

The State had already called several witnesses to lay the foundation for Johnny Long's testimony. The arresting officer told of Johnny's arrest and his immediate implication of Henry Waller. In addition to Sheriff Phillips, two other deputies told of Johnny's signed confession and his obvious fear of Henry Waller. Each seemed to have a similar impression of Johnny. They described him as a "scared kid." and a "timid boy with a slight build."

Finally, it was time for the star witness.

"The prosecution calls Johnny Long to the stand."

Johnny took short, uneasy steps up to the jury box, while Henry Waller's cold, hard eyes bore a hole into Johnny's back. Johnny appeared timid and weak as he slowly climbed onto the witness seat. His appearance was evidence of the unmistakable toll of having spent the last few months in jail. He looked like a frail, frightened teenager. His eyes were wide with dread and panic. He was unsure of himself as he took the stand. His small stature on the stand and his simple attire were very much befitting of an innocent county boy, far outside of his comfort zone. Nevertheless, Johnny had seen a lot and he knew a lot. It was the prosecution's job to get him to tell that story now.

Raising his right hand, Johnny swore to tell the truth, as he carefully avoided looking at Henry. He could feel the threats emitting from every fiber of Henry's being even though he was fifteen feet away. Wanting to disappear into thin air, Johnny took a deep breath and tried to focus on the prosecution. Johnny had endured many meetings with the prosecution's team. He knew what they would ask of him. His attorney had prepped him for the possible challenges that would come from the defense. He hated the position he was in. He did not want to face Henry, or the members of his family who sat in the courtroom. He just wanted to disappear.

Johnny's initial questions were tranquil enough. What was his name and age? What was his usual place of residence? What did he do for a living? Then came the questions that he was dreading.

"Are you acquainted with the defendant in this case?"

"Yes, sir."

"And how are you acquainted with the defendant?"

"Me and my sister Eva lived on his place in Germantown. I worked for him from time to time."

"Can you tell us where you were on the evening of December 24, 1916?"

"I was at my parent's house that evening. We was celebratin' Christmas Eve. Me and my family was fiddling, and singing Christmas songs 'til pert near midnight."

"After awhile, I headed for bed in the room with my brothers."

"Did you go right to sleep?"

"No, Sir." he stated. "I waited for muh brothers to fall asleep and then I snuck out the house. I rounded up my brother's horse and headed back to Grove."

"So, it's well after midnight, and you round up a horse in the dark of night and ride back to Grove. What on earth would make you leave your cozy home on Christmas Eve and go back to Grove?" the attorney feigned surprise.

"I was afraid not to go. Henry said he would be waitin and that I had better go."

"Did Mr. Waller say what the two of you would do when you arrived at Grove?"

"Yes Sir. He said that we would pick up the negroes Chester and Mark and go to Old Man Reeves place."

"Objection!" your Honor.

"Overruled!"

"And did Henry say why he wanted to go to the Reeves house that night?"

"Yes, Sir, Henry come to me and said that the old man had a wad of cash. Said we were gonna take it off him."

"And how did he plan to, as you say, "Take it off him?""

"Henry had it all set up. He told me that he had a plan and I'd better go along with it. Said he'd kill me if I didn't. Said he was gonna get what the old man owed him."

"Did Mr. Waller give you details about the plan?"

"Not really. He just said that he would look out for me and I wouldn't get in any trouble."

"But he did give you some detail, did he not?"

"Well, he did tell me that if I did exactly what he wanted me to do, that neither one of us would get in no trouble. Then he told me that we would both have alibis set up. He said he'd fix it so that the negroes would take the blame."

"And how did he intend for the negroes to, as you say 'take the blame'?"

Johnny had been prepped for his testimony. He recounted the details that he had put in his confession, careful to stick to the basics.

"Henry had calculated the amount of time that we needed for the whole thing. He said that me and him would both spend the night in different places far away from Grove, so nobody would suspect us. When the time came, I was s'posed to meet him in Grove."

"And how, exactly, would that implicate the negroes?"

"Well, Henry said that he would see to it that everything we done would point to the negroes. He said that they lived close enough to Old

Man Reeves for it to all fit. Henry said that nobody would doubt that the negroes done it.

"So if Henry had the negroes to blame, why did he need you?"

"Henry said that the negroes wouldn't be suspicious of nothin if I came along because of me being friendly with 'em and all. Said they would be more amenable to comin' if I was with 'em. Henry had it all figured out."

"Objection, your Honor!"

"Sustained. Jury will ignore the last statement."

"So, you made those arrangements to meet Henry Waller"

"Yes Sir."

"Can you tell us what happened when you arrived at Chester Tyson's home?"

"Well," Johnny began. "I kinda hung back and Henry did the talkin. But I heard Chester say that he didn't want to go. But Henry kept at him. I heard him say, "You'll do as I say, Boy! And I knew Chester was scared of him, and…"

"Objection, your Honor!" Robertson was on his feet. "Objection! This witness has no first-hand knowledge of what was in the mind of Chester Tyson."

"Sustained. The jury will ignore the last statement." the judge admonished.

"Did you hear any more of the conversation between Henry and Chester?" Drew asked.

"Yes, Sir. I heard Henry say, 'you're coming with me or else! Then Chester hung his head and said, 'yes'm Boss'. Then he went back in the house and came out a few minutes later."

"Was Chester armed? Was he carrying anything?"

"I didn't see him holdin' nothin'. But when we passed by the old tree stump, Henry tol' him to grab the ax outa the stump."

"What happened next?"

"I headed up ahead of 'em to Mark Peter's house and Chester and Henry was behind me. They got there a minute or two after I did. Mark and Larkin come out da house, and Henry badgered 'em until they agreed to come with us to Old Man Reeves."

"Objection, your Honor!"

"Overruled."

"And what happened when you got to the Reeves house?"

Johnny's heart began to race as he thought back to that dreadful night. It had been the most horrible night of his life. He didn't want to relive it. Especially in a courtroom where some in attendance were family, and others whom he considered to be his closest friends. He took a deep breath, carefully avoiding any eyes that were familiar or threatening.

"When we got to the house, Henry started ordering everyone around. He took the ax from Chester and told Chester to stay by the door. He told me and Mark to come in the house with him, so we followed him in."

"What happened next?"

Johnny paused, his mind flashing to the next moments. It had been swift. And it had been brutal. Tears began to fill Johnny's eyes. He couldn't find his words.

"Mr. Long, do you need a moment? Water perhaps? Just take your time and tell us what you saw." His voice was soothing and Johnny took a deep breath and pressed on.

The crowd was on the edge of their seats as Johnny described what he had seen. He described how terrified he was when Henry quickly raised the ax against John Nelson Reeves and brought it crashing back down in the center of his skull. He relived the horror he felt when Henry

Waller went after the children who were awakened by the noise. And he told of his state of shock when Maude Reeves darted out of the house, past Johnny, with Henry at her heels. He spoke of being temporarily frozen in place and suspended in time with his mind shrouded in disbelief.

Johnny was in tears when he finally finished. He couldn't get the images of the children out of his mind, and he remembered Henry coolly washing his hands in a bucket of water, while threatening them all to keep their mouths shut, less they suffer the same fate.

"Where was the ax when Henry was washing his hands in the bucket?" the prosecuting attorney asked.

"He give it to Chester and told him to get rid of it."

"Did you see him give anything else to Chester?"

"Yes, Sir. He pulled out a pistol shoved it in Chester's chest. He laughed cause Chester shut his eyes tight like he was waitin' to be shot. He told Chester to get rid of it if he knew what was best."

"What was Chester's reaction to that?" Drew asked.

"Chester didn't say nothin. He just put in in his pocket."

"Did the negroes leave at that time?"

"We all left. Henry and me walked off in one direction, and Chester and the other negroes went in the other direction. Henry had told em to go on home. Then me and Henry separated and I went and got muh horse."

"Now, Johnny, when the Sheriff arrested you the following day did you relay the same story to him?"

"Yes, Sir."

"But if you were so afraid of Henry Waller, why did you confess?"

"Because my conscience was bothering me something awful and I needed to get it off my chest. I kept thinking about Miss Maudie and them children."

"No further questions your Honor."

Relieved that it was over Johnny took a deep breath. However, his relief was short lived.

"Mr. Robertson, do you have questions for this witness?" asked the Judge.

"Yes, your Honor!" Mr. Robertson rose to his feet. "I certainly do!"

"Mr. Long," Mr. Robertson began. "Aside from statements you made to the deputies and the Sheriff, have you told anyone else what happened on Christmas Eve of 1916?"

"No, Sir."

"Did you write anyone any letters about what happened that night?"

"Yes, Sir. I wrote a letter to my parents while I was in the Minden jail."

"And in that letter, did you admit to any involvement in the crime?"

"No Sir, I told them I wasn't involved because I didn't want them to think bad about me. Most of that letter wasn't even true."

"Are you in the habit of lying so that people won't think badly about you, Mr. Long?"

"No Sir!" a rattled Johnny pleaded. "None of that was my fault and I didn't want to take the blame for it. Me and the negroes went along with Henry because we was scared not to."

"You were afraid *not* to?" he repeated. "Didn't you just testify that you lived with Henry Waller? If you were so afraid of him, why would you live with him?"

"Me and my sister Eva needed the work." Johnny replied.

"And Henry Waller was kind enough to take you in?" he asked.

"Yes, Sir."

"What was your relationship with the negroes?" he asked.

"Well, I knew 'em since we was kids, them livin' nearby and all."

"Would you describe your relationship as close?"

"No sir, we wasn't close a'tall" replied Johnny. "We mighta worked together a time or two, but I wouldn't say we was close."

"Did you ever interact with them socially?"

"Not really. When we were kids we'd see each other sometimes but not regular."

"But didn't you just testify that Henry needed you because you were friendly with the negroes. Didn't you in fact play cards with them from time to time?"

"But we wasn't all that friendly. A lot uh people played cards together that didn't even know each other. I didn't have much to do with 'em socially."

"But you were close enough with them to call them your friends, were you not? As a matter of fact, you wrote to your parents that you were upset with the negroes isn't that correct? Didn't you have a cordial relationship with them prior to the night in question?" attorney Robertson turned to the bench.

"Your Honor, I would like to re-introduce this letter written by Mr. Long to his parents in January of this year. Now, Mr. Long, can you read for the jury, the parts of the letter that I have marked here." he said pointing to the letter as he placed it before Johnny.

Squinting his eyes to make out his own writing, Johnny began to read.

"I have found out now that it won't do to have anything to do with a Negro for if they ever get in any trouble themselves they will bring you in just as sure as you are living they will do it. I am going to be sent to the pen on a count of it. Just as sure as the world stands that will be awful to have to go on the count of a stankin god dam black negro. If I ever get out of the pen I am going to when a negro asks me for anything I am going to hall away and knock the hell right out of him just as soon as he asks me." Johnny finished reading and looked up at Attorney Robertson.

"Mr. Long," Attorney Robertson continued. "Were you upset with the negroes because the agreement that you had with them to frame Henry Waller had fallen apart and...."

"Objection, your Honor!"

"Sustained."

"Mr. Long. Did you attempt to hire an automobile for yourself and the negroes on the night in question?"

"That was Henry's plan! Henry had wanted me to hire a motor-car and I told him that I..."

"Objection your Honor! I object to this entire line of questioning!"

"Please approach the bench!" Judge Sandlin directed the two attorneys who were now shouting over each other.

When they returned, the Mr. Robertson only had a few simple questions for Johnny. Whatever the Judge had said to him must have made quite an impact.

Johnny was relieved when he finished. Finally, he was allowed to step down from the stand.

During a brief recess, the courtroom was abuzz with the revelations heard during Johnny's questioning. Most of the spectators believed Johnny. He did not appear to be a hardened criminal. In fact, he reminded many of them of their own children and they felt sorry for him. He seemed anguished and lost.

They milled about the courtroom wondering who the bailiff would call next. They dashed back to their seats when he opened the side door. The courtroom was quiet with anticipation as the bailiff spoke. "All rise!" he ordered.

After Judge Sandlin entered the courtroom and took his seat, they sat down and fixed their eyes on the side door, straining to get the first glimpse of the next witness. Excitement arose upon the announcement.

"The people would like to call Mark Peters."

"Mark sauntered into the courtroom refusing show any fear or intimidation towards a room full of white folks. He was steadfast and confident as he gave his testimony. Twice, the prosecution asked him who killed John Reeves. And twice he pointed Henry Waller out as the ax-wielding killer!

His testimony was the same one he had given at his own trial. However, this time, it was supported and strengthened by Johnny Long's account of the murders. Although he visibly stiffened at the call for re-direct from the defense, he did not waver in his testimony. If anything, he was more assured than ever in his answers. When he finished, he sauntered back out of the courtroom, taking just an extra second to mock Henry Waller.

All eyes were on the bailiff as he called the next witness.

"The people would like to call Chester Tyson."

Chester entered the courtroom, his eyes cold and looking every bit like the condemned man that he was. Months of being in prison and on death row had taken a toll on his body and had hardened his soul. He took the stand knowing that everything that could have been done to him already had been. He would hang soon. And the bastard responsible for it sat just out of his reach. Damn him! Chester might be headed to the gallows but he was hell bent on taking Henry Waller with him!

Chester was filled with anger and hate. With his shoulders squared, he glanced over the spectators that filled the courtroom. It was clearly a white man's arena. A certain decorum was evident, that had not been present at his own trial. His so-called "defense" attorney D. Webster Stewart was sitting near the front, straight up despite his advancing age.

Waller's attorney presented a sharp and on point defense, appearing ready to pounce at the slightest hint of impropriety. Each juror had a notepad in front of him, pencils poised to take meaningful notes. And, unlike the jurors at Chester's trial, numerous pages had already been turned, indicating the countless details taken by each juror thus far.

However, even with all of the visible changes, the biggest difference by far in Chester's mind, was the fact that Johnny Long, star witness for the Henry Waller defense, had not testified at Chester's trial. Although they did not speak, Chester had seen Johnny while he was waiting to be called. Word was out that Johnny would testify and point the finger at Waller. Johnny had not been called to do that on Chester's behalf or on behalf of any of the others during the first trial. Chester was certain that they hadn't wanted to waste a white man on a Negro trial. Johnny could have told the jury that Waller forced them to go. He could have saved them from the gallows or possibly even a conviction. Of course, Johnny probably would have been afraid to point the finger at a white man during a Negro trial. He would have very well been placing his own life on the line. On second thought, even if Johnny had testified, the jury would have had to care. And clearly, they did not.

Chester looked directly into Henry Waller's eyes. Unlike Johnny's testimony, no tears flowed from Chester's eyes. Henry Waller stared right back at Chester. He was not intimidated. Even from the defense table, his eyes were threatening Chester. Chester could read the meaning behind them, Henry daring Chester to tell what he knew. But it didn't matter to Chester. He coldly matched Henry Waller's stare! Chester couldn't wait to point the finger at Henry.

He very quickly got that chance. He gave much of the same testimony that he had given at his own trial. But this time he was allowed to invoke the name of Henry Waller. When asked if he saw the man in the courtroom who had come to his home that fateful night, his hand was steady and his voice was firm.

"Yes, Sir!" he stated emphatically as he pointed to Henry Waller. "That man sitting right there! It was him! It was Henry Waller who came to my door, and forced me to go!"

"Objection, your honor!"

"Overruled!" the judge stated, admonishing Chester to keep his answers tailored to the questions.

A little later, he got a chance to once more stick it to Henry, when asked if he saw anyone strike Maude Reeves.

"Yes, Sir!" I saw Henry Waller chase Miss Maudie with the ax. I saw him raise it against her, and I heard him boast that he had killed her!"

"Objection, your Honor!"

"Overruled!" Sandlin bellowed.

"Satisfied, Chester sat back in his seat as Henry Waller shot daggers at him with his eyes.

Chester and Mark had accomplished what they had set out to do. Both knew that the white folks expected them to be downtrodden and intimidated in the white man's courtroom. Both were rigidly examined and cross-examined. However, neither of them broke down, or became tangled up in their answers.

Four heavily armed deputies escorted them out of the courtroom amid a crowd of curious onlookers. Some just wanted to get a look at the convicted killers. Others had a clear message for them; "Die Nigger!"

While Chester and Mark were on the train headed back to their dungeons, the prosecution rested its case. After a brief lunch, the court reconvened for the defense to present its case.

The defense jumped at its chance to scrub Henry Waller clean while Chester and Mark headed back to the penitentiary.

"He was friendly and light-hearted." friends testified to Henry Waller's personality. His friends and relatives issued glowing reports about his "stellar" character. His brothers described him as a loving father and a good friend to others. Close neighbors described him as someone who was always willing to lend a helping hand to others in need. Henry beamed at his 10-year-old son, Tom Waller, playing every bit the part of a loving father, as the glowing comments flooded in about his "good moral fabric".

Next, the testimony turned to Henry's whereabouts that fateful night. One witness after another testified to seeing him late on Christmas Eve and early on Christmas day.

"Yep, they were headed in the direction of Serepta." offered Ben Wren.

" Why, I saw him and his brother and children pass right by my house on Christmas Eve," swore Miss Mamie Withers, postmistress for Grove. "They were headed in the direction of Minden."

District Attorney Drew's rigorous cross-examination failed to cause any of them to change their stories.

"He was with me Christmas Eve." We went to Serepta and saw the Widow Krouse. He gave her a Christmas gift. Then we saw Ben Wren along the way." stated Henry's brother, Whit Waller. "We didn't get to my brother Jesse's house up near Serepta till 'bout 8:00 that night. We stayed there an hour and then went to Walter Dean's house 'til pert near 11."

"Mr. Dean, when did you next see Henry?"

"Well, I saw him again on Christmas morning about daylight when he came over to get a drink."

"Did you serve him that drink, Mr. Dean?"

"Yes, sir."

"I'm curious Mr. Dean, what did Henry Waller drink that morning? Coffee? Water?"

"Whiskey, straight."

"Just one?"

"Maybe two. I don't remember."

"Are you in the habit of serving whiskey to guests that early in the morning?" inquired Drew.

"Well, it was not unusual for Henry." was Mr. Dean's answer.

"No further questions of this witness."

The defense had managed to account for Henry's time all day Christmas Eve and up to about eleven-thirty that night.

Accounting for Henry's hours between eleven-thirty that night and about 7:30 the next morning proved a bit more problematic.

For the hours they could not account for, they took great pains to show that it was impossible for Henry to murder a family and make it back home within that limited time frame.

Next, Jim Long, brother of Johnny Long, testified that he nailed Johnny's horse in a stable to keep him from getting out and turned his own horse loose in the pasture. His attempt to protect Johnny and show that he could not have easily caught his horse failed, when upon cross-examination he admitted that two little boys had very quickly caught his horse later that same week.

And although both Henry's and Johnny's relatives had testified to seeing them go to bed on Christmas Eve, no one could say with certainty that they did not get out of bed and leave.

When testimony turned to the distance of travel between Serepta and Grove, the defense aimed to prove that the distance was too great to accomplish the given crime and return to Serepta within the amount of time of which Henry was unaccounted.

Witnesses were called to testify to the fact that no ordinary horse could make it from Serepta to Grove and back without great harm and fatigue over the wee midnight hours.

They presented a carefully mapped out a re-enactment of Waller's movements complete with time stamps and details of what they called a "difficult terrain than existed that night." They attempted to show that the chosen mode of transportation – horseback – would have been an incredible undertaking that night because no horse could elicit the stamina it would take to complete such a trip in such a short amount of time. "Therefore", they concluded, "It would have been impossible for Henry Waller to have committed the murders because it would have been physically impossible for him to have been seen near midnight on Christmas Eve, committed murder, and be seen again at 7:30 in the morning on Christmas Day.

Not to be outdone, the prosecution vigorously cross-examined, often showing by the defense' own witnesses that the trip could be made with hours to spare. And he drove home the point that there were automobile tracks around the property whose owners had not been identified, and that Johnny had been asked to hire a motor car.

"An average horse could make the trip within hours with no problem or harm to the horse." was the next testimony of several witnesses.

Additionally, the prosecution managed to impeach several defense witnesses by showing that Henry Waller's brother had talked to several witnesses in the case and compared notes as to their upcoming testimony.

At the end of the day, both hoped that they had swayed the jury enough to cause reasonable doubt. The Court recessed at 6:30 pm.

The next day, Waller decided to try to save his own neck. He would testify on his own behalf.

It was not something that his attorney's wanted, however, Waller was confident in his own charm, and against their warnings, he decided to proceed. Henry Waller's attorney's kept their questions brief, so as not to open the door to challenges by the prosecution. Henry's actual testimony was limited to just a few questions and only lasted ten minutes.

"Where were you on Sunday afternoon?"

"I spent the night at the home of my brother, Jesse Waller."

"When did you hear about the crime?

"Monday night at a Christmas tree in Evergreen."

But moments later, the prosecution had their shot at Henry Waller.

"Did you not telephone Sheriff Phillips on Tuesday night and say that you had 'just heard' about the murders?" Foster asked attempting to impeach Waller's testimony.

"Objection your Honor!" Robertson rose to his feet.

"Over-ruled!"

"I did call the Sheriff and might have said Tuesday, but I meant to say I heard Monday."

"Are you guilty of the Reeves murders?"

"I am absolutely innocent!"

With that, Henry Waller's testimony was over.

CHAPTER 10

THE WALLER VERDICT

There was a stark contrast between closing arguments in Henry Waller's trial, and closing arguments in the "Negro" trial. In the latter, the entire trial, including jury selection had taken only a day. After little more than an hour the following day, Chester Tyson and Mark Peters had received a death sentence, and Larkin Stewart and Anderson Heard had received life imprisonment.

After Henry Waller's trial, each side was given two hours with which to make their closing arguments. Those closing arguments were thorough, full of details, and passionately delivered on both sides.

The prosecution was very aggressive in its approach.

"Gentlemen of the jury," attorney Harmon Drew began. "Henry Waller would have us believe that he is an innocent man incapable of committing this heinous crime. But Henry Waller has a history of violence. Testimony has shown that Henry Waller had not only the motive; but he had both the means and the opportunity to leave Serepta on a quiet Christmas Eve, viciously kill five members of an innocent family, and return to Serepta on Christmas day, feeling festive and good about his dastardly deeds. Now, let's look at the motive. Testimony has shown that Mr. Waller threatened violence against Mr. Reeves on at least two occasions. They had a very contentious past. Prior to the murders, the victim, John Nelson Reeves had evidence of a crime committed by Henry Waller that would have put Mr. Waller away for a very long time and Henry Waller wanted to silence him. Henry also knew that John Nelson Reeves might have shared that information with his wife, the late Maude

153

Reeves. So, he devised a plan. He would kill them both and make it look like a robbery. You might wonder why he killed the children. After all, they would not have been able to articulate the crime. They were too young. In fact, the youngest victim was only 18 months old. But they were awakened by the noise of death, and Henry knew that the older children could identify him. And sheer malice led him to take out his rage on anyone in the family. So he took an ax and hacked them all to death." he said, carefully emphasizing each word.

"Now, what about opportunity?" he continued. "Henry Waller would have us believe that he was nowhere near Grove at the time the murders took place. The defense has brought forth a parade of witnesses to testify to the fact that he was in Serepta both the night before the murders and the morning after. These witnesses all provided Henry with a carefully crafted alibi. Henry Waller took great pains to parade through town to make sure that he was seen as late as possible on December 24th, and as early as possible on December 25th. Most of those witnesses would have you believe that it would have been impossible for Henry to leave Serepta on Christmas Eve and be seen again early in the morning on Christmas day. They have testified to Mr. Waller's gay demeanor as he celebrated with his family around a Christmas Tree. But all of Henry's actions were carefully planned. And they were carefully executed.

Gentlemen of the jury, let's turn your attention to several of our expert witnesses. These expert witnesses have testified that not only would it have been *possible* for Henry Waller to ride a horse that night, maliciously execute a family in the most monstrous manner known to man and return to Serepta within hours; they testified that it would be an easy feat for any normal horse. And let us not forget the testimony of Johnny Long, gentlemen. You heard Johnny's letter that mentions hiring a motor car. A drive from Serepta to Grove and back in a motor car could be easily accomplished without detection in the wee hours of the morning. And most importantly, ladies and gentlemen, even though Henry Waller would tell you that no one saw him that night, we have testimony that shows otherwise. Henry Waller was seen by Chester Tyson, Mark Peters, and, and Johnny Long. All three of those men have given you detailed accounts not only of Henry's whereabouts during those "unseen" hours, but also of his reprehensible actions that night. These men had no opportunity to consult with one another before giving their *sworn* statements. And gentlemen each of those statements included identical and minute details about Henry Waller's actions that night. And lest we forget" he said looking directly at the jury as he lowered his voice. "Henry Waller was seen by several *other* people that night. He was seen by Mr. John Nelson Reeves as he hacked his body into pieces. He was seen by little David Reeves and by baby Alto Reeves as he stood over their little bodies and brought an ax crashing down upon them. And he was seen by Mrs. Maude Reeves, who, just after seeing him kill her husband and children, looked directly into his eyes and attempted to flee from death." he said slowly and deliberately. "Those people," he said gently. "cannot be here to testify, because they are dead at the hands of Henry Waller!" He paused briefly to let the thought sink in, and then he continued.

"An ax, ladies and gentlemen." he stated, allowing time for the image to linger on the jury's minds. "An ax was Henry Waller's means for carrying out this horrible crime. Henry Waller carefully chose a weapon that he knew would be traced to someone else. After forcing Chester Tyson to bring this weapon, Henry Waller committed murder with it, and then gave it back to Chester Tyson to dispose of it. He knew all along that the weapon would be linked to Mr. Tyson. And after Henry Waller's killing spree was over, five innocent people lay dead, and Henry Waller went about his merry way."

"Gentlemen, the people of this great State ask that you find Henry Waller guilty of murder in the first degree, and ensure that he pay for these awful crimes. We ask you to return a verdict of "guilty with capital punishment!"

After a brief recess, the defense took its turn at the jury. Attorney Robertson's voice was even more passionate than the prosecution's.

"Gentlemen of the jury" he began. "The prosecution has told you a fascinating tale. The only problem though, is that none of it is true."

"Are we actually to believe that Mr. Henry Waller, a hardworking, upstanding man with respected ties to this community would actually commit such a horrible crime?" he asked incredulously.

"To be sure, gentlemen," he continued, "Someone with evil in their heart and an ax in their hand, did take the lives of five innocent people on that fateful night. But it was not my client, Mr. Henry Waller!" he said nodding in the direction of the defense table.

"Although the prosecution dwells on the fact that Mr. Waller's own relatives testified in mass about seeing him on Christmas Eve and Christmas day, they were not the only ones to do so. The postmistress of this great Parish testified to seeing him and reported that nothing seemed to be amiss. People who have never laid eyes on Henry Waller testified to seeing him pass and exchanging pleasantries. Mr. Waller's focus that night was to simply spend time with his family over Christmas." He said, emphasizing the season.

His brother and other members of his family saw him go to bed that night. Wouldn't the quietness of the hour awaken at least one person in that small house if Henry had attempted to leave? And what about the distance between Serepta and Grove, and the conditions that night? Witnesses testified that the rough terrain would have delayed and tired even the best horse," he boomed. "And when that idea fails, the prosecution attempts to trick you by bringing forth the preposterous idea that Mr. Waller could have hired an automobile that night, right? But not one witness testified that Mr. Waller approached them about hiring an automobile. The only mention of hiring an automobile came from a letter written by Johnny Long to his parents. Johnny himself admitted that most of that letter was made up of lies and fabrications. In fact, testimony has shown that Johnny Long told many lies both under oath and to his friends and family. So now, we are to believe that Johnny Long told the truth about an automobile? That is ludicrous gentlemen!" he said mocking the very idea.

Robertson strolled to the other side of the jury box. "And what about motive, gentlemen?" he began. "An argument? Are we to believe that a simple argument between two friends would cause one man to kill an entire family? Even if some dastardly soul is vicious enough to do that, Henry Waller certainly is not! Henry Waller and John Nelson Reeves had been friends for years. Their friendship had already withstood the test of time. Like most of us with close friends, there is bound to be a disagreement or two. But to rise to the level of taking not only your *friend's* life, but also the life of his wife and children? No, gentlemen, this is not the work of someone who called Mr. Reeves their friend. This is the work of a deranged and immoral mind!" He said with conviction.

"Now, gentlemen, let's talk about the weapon." The Reeves family was killed with Chester Tyson's ax. Many people knew that Chester Tyson and his acquaintances frequently used this ax. Chester Tyson was found at his home, with John Reeves pistol hidden underneath his mattress. Gentlemen, it is a known fact that there was no love lost between Chester Tyson and John Reeves. But the prosecution would have you believe that my client planned out and executed an entire family murder but gave no forethought to what weapon he was going use?" he said shaking his head. "Doesn't that defy logic for someone who was supposedly cunning enough to plan out every minute of an entire day?" he bellowed letting the thought linger.

"Mr. Waller was in Serepta celebrating Christmas with his family at the time of the murders." he continued. He had no grudge against the Reeves family that would cause him to even entertain such a crime. Mr. Waller is a victim of a shrewd plan by a group of people who wanted to frame him for something that he would never do. Gentlemen of the jury, the prosecution has attempted to place doubt about this man into your minds. There is no way that any reasonable person could conclude that my client is guilty. Therefore, gentlemen, we ask that you do the right thing and let this man resume his rightful place with his son and his family. We ask that you take a sensible approach to the testimony heard during this trial and that you find Mr. Henry Waller, 'Not Guilty' of these horrific crimes!"

With that, closing arguments concluded and the jury received its instructions late that evening.

Reporters milled about the courthouse, wanting to be the first to hear the news. Mariah and Georgia sat at home, waiting for someone to bring news about the trial. They hoped that Henry Waller would be found guilty, and subsequently their sons would be found innocent and be allowed to come home. When the jury failed to reach a verdict that evening, the spectators returned early the following morning to be in place when it happened. People moved in and out of the courtroom, hoping to have a front row seat when the Judge announced the verdict.

At four o'clock the following day, the jury foreman knocked on the door to the courtroom and handed the bailiff a note. Notice was quickly given to all necessary participants, who rushed to the courtroom. As word spread, the courtroom quickly filled to capacity. People formed small clusters in the back and in the aisles of the courtroom. They sat on the hard benches, some facing those behind them to formulate groups for discussion.

The courtroom was abuzz with theories about the jury's decision, and the details of the crime. The last few months had given them much to consider and during Henry Waller's trial, many reconsidered as to the guilt of the "negroes".

They had heard the evidence. Many of them knew Henry Waller personally. Regardless of what his family had said, Henry was no saint. He was known to be a drunk. And a mean drunk at that. People who knew him said that he was mean and cunning. An acquaintance once remarked that "Henry could steal the jelly out of a biscuit and not break the crust!"

Some were conflicted because they knew other members of Henry's family. Many of the other Waller's were well-respected members of the community. However, Henry was somewhat of a newcomer. He was not a long-time member of the community like his relatives. He was a recent transplant from Texas. And he had shown them no reason to respect him.

However, they did have a soft spot for Johnny Long. Johnny was a kid that many of them had known from the day he was born. He still appeared to be younger than his years, and he had seemed terrified on the witness stand. He didn't seem like someone who was either vicious enough or cunning enough to plan such a crime. No, they reasoned, it was much more likely that Johnny was a pawn of Henry Waller.

They scrambled back to their seats and sat up straight as the bailiff lead the jury back into the courtroom. They scoured the expressions of the jury for any hint of whether the jury would find Henry guilty or innocent. However, the jury appeared expressionless and gave no hint about their findings.

Finally, the Judge entered and everyone stood according to protocol, excited to be a part of this historic verdict, and interested to find out if Henry would hang.

Glancing over the papers on his desk, the Judge nodded to the jury foreman, and then turned his attention to Henry Waller.

"Mr. Waller, will you please stand to receive the verdict."

Henry Waller slowly rose to his feet. The judge then directed his next statement to the jury foreman.

"Sir, will you please stand and read the verdict?" The jury foreman stood up and faced the courtroom.

"We the jury," the foreman began. "find the defendant, Henry Waller, 'Guilty as charged but without capital punishment in the murder of Maude Reeves."

Contrary to prior instructions from the Judge, the courtroom buzzed with excitement as the other verdicts were read.

"No! God no!" cried Waller's sister from the first row. "Henry's innocent!" Henry's knuckles turned white as he tightly gripped the edge of the table. Tears streamed down his cheeks as his mind grasped the news.

"Mr. Waller, would you please remain standing?" the Judge directed.

Shocked by the verdict, Henry had leaned over and had placed both hands on the table to steady himself. Now, in response to Judge Sandlin's request, he let go of the table with one hand, and finally feeling that he could stand on his own two feet, he let go o f the table with the other hand. On wobbly knees, a tearful Henry stood and faced the judge.

"Mr. Waller, you have been found guilty as charged, but without capital punishment for the murders of Maude Reeves and John Nelson Reeves. Do you have anything that you would like to say before I pass sentence in this case?"

"Yes, your Honor." Henry said his voice barely about a whisper.

"Your Honor," Henry began, his voice still shaky but a bit louder this time. "I am not guilty of these crimes. Your Honor, you can't send me to prison for something someone else did, Sir. I have a son that depends on me. Please, your Honor! Please!"

His sister, Mrs. Walter Dean began to wail. "Henry's voice began to crack and he became even more emotional as his sister sobbed. Out of the corner of his eye, he saw his brothers, Dr. L.T. Waller, Jessie Waller and Reed Waller, trying to comfort her. He fought back the tears as he continued to try to reason with the Judge.

"Your Honor, I swear to you I am innocent! I'm innocent!" he repeated, sobbing. Overcome by emotion, he began to slump back down into his chair, and attempted to stabilize his shaking knees. Flanked by his attorney's one on either side of him, he once again steadied himself and leaned against the table. The buzz in the courtroom became louder as everyone reacted to Henry's emotional breakdown.

"Quiet!" the Judge banged his gavel on the block as he tried to restore calm to the courtroom. "Order! Order in the court!"

Finally, the courtroom settled down, and the Judge once again turned his attention to the defendant.

"Mr. Henry Waller," by reason of the law and the evidence against you, this jury has found you "Guilty as Charged, of murder in the first degree without capital punishment. As to your convictions by this jury today, it is ordered, adjudged and decreed that as the defendant for these crimes, you shall be confined at hard labor in the Louisiana State Prison for a period of your natural life. It is so ordered!"

"Henry finally collapsed onto the chair beneath him." It was bad enough to be found guilty. It was even worse to hear that he would be sent to Angola Prison. He remembered hearing that nothing was worse than doing time at the *Farm*. At that point, his attorney sprang into action!

"Your Honor," Robertson stated. "At this time the defense would like to move for judgement notwithstanding the verdict. We reserve this bill as a matter of law. There was no evidence presented by which this sentence should stand." he continued.

" You certainly have that right, Mr. Robertson." Motion denied."

" Your Honor," Robertson continued. "The defense moves for appeal."

"Duly noted." was the response from the Judge.

Two guards led Henry from the courtroom and took him back to the Webster Parish jail. There, he would await his transfer to The Louisiana State Penitentiary in Angola, Louisiana. He would take up residence at the same place where Chester Tyson and the other colored men were serving time for the murders of Maude Reeves and John Nelson Reeves. However, there was little chance of Henry laying eyes on any of the four colored men. It was 1917 and the prison, was segregated. If Henry was thankful for anything, it was that he did not have to be confronted by four angry colored men, doing time for murder.

Henry didn't have to worry. Chester and the others soon had other things on their minds. They had heard about Henry's conviction. Their focus now, was to use that fact to try to get their own convictions over-turned. Chester knew that Henry had appealed. Therefore, Henry still had a chance of going free. All Chester could hope for was commutation, and he knew that the chances of that were slim. Convicts rarely prevailed when fighting for release. Especially colored convicts.

Chester Tyson mulled over his situation. Death Row. Convicted Killer. Murderer. As he lay on his cold, hard, bunk, all of the awful terms circled around in his head. He had settled into Angola Prison, fully expecting to be there until they wrapped that rope around his neck and he dangled from the gallows. But he wouldn't go down without a fight. If nothing else, he wanted his family to know that he didn't kill those people. He had appealed to the Pardon Board to review his case, and he was waiting to hear their decision.

Unbeknownst to Chester, his chances had improved considerably. The tide of public opinion had shifted after Waller's trial, and hundreds of people, black and white, felt that the colored men had been railroaded by Henry Waller. They felt that they should not die for a murder that another man committed. Consequently, many petitions and letters had been written on their behalf to Governor Pleasant and the pardon board. However, opinions on the matter were strong, and mixed. Some felt that their convictions should be immediately and completely overturned.

"They were forced to go at gunpoint! They were dupes of those conniving white men!" They reasoned. "They had no clue what would happen when they got there. They should let them go."

Others were more cautious in their reasoning.

"Well, they *were* at the scene," they admonished. "They had to know *something*! They shouldn't have been there at all. Maybe they shouldn't hang, but they should stay in prison."

The prevailing thought was that the "negroes" had paid too high a price for their involvement in the crime, and that Henry Waller had paid too little. They wanted Henry Waller to hang!

Henry was well aware that the tide was turning against him. Although most of the lynchings taking place in Louisiana during that time were colored men, it did not escape him that several white men were lynched for crimes far less than his. His self-assured cockiness did not serve him well at Angola. Although he had filed an appeal in his case, his attorney advised him that he had only been tried on two of the five indictments that had been returned against him. The state held back on trying him for the murders of the Reeves children so that there would be another avenue, to try him on other charges if more evidence came to light. Henry knew, that unlike the first jury, there was no guarantee that the next jury wouldn't decide to hang him if he was found guilty. He assessed his options, and on March 24, 1917, only a few weeks after his conviction, he formally withdrew his appeal and accepted his sentence of "life" in the penitentiary. The prosecution agreed to pass on the remaining charges of murder that were pending against him but they reserved the right to try him again if a material change in the case developed. Little did Henry know that the prosecution was continuing with vigor to re-develop a case against him so that they could quell that outrage that had taken over Minden, and the surrounding Parishes in Louisiana. "Damn Johnny Long!" Henry simmered. "If only he had kept his mouth shut!"

Johnny still had his own charges to deal with. The prosecution had cut a deal with him and he had decided to plead guilty for complicity in the murder of John and Maude Reeves, as well as their three children. On June 20, 1917 Johnny went before the Judge. The prosecution advised him that they couldn't promise him release, but that the Judge might go easy on him because of his age, and his previous testimony at Henry's trial.

After Johnny's guilty plea the judge gave him an opportunity to make a statement in his own behalf. Johnny gave it his all, but during his statement, he admitted to several things that he had omitted at the Waller trial. In his attempt to impress upon the judge that Henry was the only one responsible, Johnny admitted that Henry had involved him early on. He admitted that he knew not only about the possibility of a robbery, but that Henry had given him many other details. He knew that Henry planned to use an ax to kill the Reeves because he felt that no one would connect him with it. And he knew where Chester kept his ax. In Johnny's rambling attempt to justify his involvement, he told the Judge that Henry told him to set up an own alibi. He admitted that Henry trusted him to figure out his own alibi, saying that Christmas would be an easy time to do it.

When asked what he had to say before sentence was passed, Johnny made a short statement and appealed for a pardon based on the fact that he had been instrumental in bringing Waller to justice. He completed his statement saying, "Your Honor, I was in it and I will take my medicine like a man."

Johnny's statements earned him a conviction of "Life" at the Louisiana State Prison." He would not face the death penalty. He would serve his time along with Henry Waller at "The Farm." On June 20, 1917, Johnny began his sentence for his part in the murder of the Reeves family.

After Johnny's conviction, people in the surrounding parts of Louisiana, and even many in other states, became increasingly outraged at the fact that Johnny and Henry were only serving life sentences, while Chester and Mark were facing the death penalty. Black Ministers and organizations called for total pardons. They pointed to the many injustices and the numerous lynchings heaped upon the Negro population in Louisiana and they called for justice. The entire trial had been a farce, they said. The trial of all four negroes had taken place in a single day. They pointed to the lackluster defense by D. Webster Stewart, and argued that his actions amounted to malpractice The jury was privy to pre-trial publicity, and was inattentive, and operated with methods that were without basis in the law. They cited the failure to call Johnny Long, the only white man who had pertinent details that were necessary to tell the whole story. They argued that Johnny's testimony was a much-needed piece for the jury to make an informed decision.

They pointed out that Johnny had provided written statements pointing to Henry Waller long before the trial took place. He could have identified the real instigator of the crime, possibly saving them from conviction.

And they wrote that, unlike Henry Waller, the colored men were not afforded the means to appeal the verdict. They commented that injustice was quick and complete. They stated that had the negro trial and the white trial been conducted in the same manner, they might not have been convicted at all, more-less given the death penalty. Their voices, which had been strong all along, beginning with the wholesale rounding up of all of the colored men in Grove, were now even stronger given the support of the white citizens that joined them in their quest for justice.

CHAPTER 11

FACING THE NOOSE

The Lyon's Club, as did many other white organizations, circulated a petition, calling for the Pardon Board to revisit the capital murder convictions of Chester Tyson and Mark Peters. Many other organizations and people in the community wrote letters to the local newspapers, the Governor, and the Pardon Board to ask them to return a decision that reflected justice.

By October, the pressure from the public was overwhelming. On October 9, 1917, Mr. D.Webster Stewart, Mark and Chester's former attorney, appealed to the pardon board on their behalf, asking that their sentence be commuted to life imprisonment. Additionally, Judge Sandlin, who had originally presided over their trial, strongly recommended that their sentences be commuted to life. He was joined in his efforts with the District Attorney Harmon Drew, who in a strongly worded opinion, wrote that the sentence should be commuted so that "if any innocent person has been made to suffer, that relief might be had for that person. Even Governor Newton C. Blanchard, the former Governor of Louisiana, wrote a letter to the Board of Pardons. *The Shreveport Times* published his letter, which read in part:

"Editor Times"

The murder of the Reeves family in Webster Parish some time ago is still fresh in our memories.

For those murders, Henry Waller and John Long, white men, and Mark Peters and Chester Tyson, negroes, were indicted. My recollection is the four men were not tried together, but that the white men were tried before one jury who found them guilty without capital punishment, while the negroes were tried later (sic) by another jury, who found them guilty as charged.

The verdict in the case of the white men carried with it, under the law the sentence of imprisonment at hard labor for life, while the verdict in the case of the colored men carried with it the death penalty.

It will be seen that the white men escaped the severest sentence of the law while on the negroes is imposed the severest penalty of the law.

…I am one of the citizens of Louisiana and their name is legion –who does not think the negroes Mark Peters and Chester Tyson ought to hang.

To hang them would be to mete out one sort of justice to the more guilty white men, Henry Waller and John Long and serve another sort of justice to the negroes, their dupes.

The white men are the more guilty because more intelligent and the belief is general that it was Waller who instigated the murders. He gets off with a life sentence, which is equivalent under our "good time" law, with only 14 or 15 years in the penitentiary, while the negroes get their necks broken.

To commute the sentence of the negroes would be to equalize justice in this case and let there be an equality of justice…."

Newton C. Blanchard, Former Governor, Louisiana

On November 8, 1917, the Board of Pardon sent its recommendation to Governor Pleasant. To the surprise of many, they asked the Governor to reduce the sentences of Chester Tyson and Mark Peters to life imprisonment.

Chester was shocked and elated that so many people cared about his plight. His hopes began to rise over the next few weeks. As he lay on his cold hard cot at night he could almost smell the aroma of his mother's delicious peach cobbler floating through the air. Visions of holding his sweetheart, Hattie in his arms filled his thoughts. He could imagine tossing a ball around with the two children that they would someday have. Their happy life would surround them day after day.

Most people were pleased the Board of Pardon's recommendation, although there were plenty of people who still wanted everyone who was involved, including Chester, Mark *and* Waller to hang.

"They are handling the whole thing backwards!" Some complained. "Instead of letting any of them murderers get off Scott free, they need to hang the whole damned lot of 'em!"

However, Mark and Chester's families were encouraged and surprised at the support. They were shocked at the former Governor's letter, and they were overjoyed when they heard the news of the Board's recommendation.

"They ain't gonna hang our boys!" they beamed. "They may even let em' go!" They began to prepare for their return. They prayed not only that Governor Pleasant would sign the Pardon Board's recommendation, but that he would also issue a complete pardon and release their loved ones soon!

Hattie was certain that she would once again have her man at home. Their baby had been born while Chester was in prison, and she made the trip to the Louisiana State Prison to let Chester know that she and the baby would be waiting for him.

When Chester learned that he had a visitor, he was very worried. He rarely had visitors at the prison because it was a long treacherous trip to make from home. Additionally, he felt that Angola was such a horrible place, that he didn't want anyone to see him there. However, Hattie thought that the trip was important.

Sitting across from him she filled him in on the latest news.

"You know that they's a whole bunch of people pushin' fo' yo' release, right?" she began. Even dat ol' judge wants 'em to release you.

"Yeah, I heard." Chester acknowledged. "But you know they ain't gonna just let us go, right?" he admonished. "We may not hang, but you know we ain't never getting out of the pen, right?" Chester didn't want her to get her hopes too high.

"I know that's what the white folks is saying, but the black folks done called in the League for the Advancement of the Colored People in New York, and they's gonna push for a full out release. They knows ya'll is innocent. You was a witness, that's all!" she insisted. "A witness! And me and this baby gonna be right here when you gits out!"

"Now don't you go gettin' your hopes up, gal." Chester cautioned. Those white folks want to see us hang. They ain't gonna stand for nothin less! Now, you go on and get on with your life. No use waitin for me. I'm gonna either be swinging by a rope, or locked up in here for the rest of *my* life.

Yet, Hattie was hopeful. She understood that Chester didn't want to get her hopes up too high, but nevertheless, she felt that he would soon be coming home.

Over the next month, Chester vacillated between feeling hopeful and feeling doomed. He tried to push possibility of a commuted sentence from his mind to avoid the profound disappointment he would feel when he learned that it was not to be. He was anxious to hear back from the parole board.

On November 27, 1917, he heard the jingling of keys turning in the lock of the heavy cell. It was after breakfast, but too early for lunch. Startled, he heard the loud booming voice of the warden.

"Come on boy!" the warden ordered. "We are going for a walk."

Puzzled, he followed the warden down the long cold corridor and into a room furnished simply with a long table and four chairs. Finally, he looked up and saw four white men sitting on the straight-back chairs. With a start, he recognized their faces. It was the Parole Board! His knees shook, as he was lead to the seat directly in front of them. He could not read their faces as the three of them fumbled with their papers on the wooden table in front of them. Finally, they put down their papers and focused their attention on Chester.

"Mr. Tyson," said the Officer on the left. As you know, this board sent a recommendation to Governor Pleasant asking him to reduce your sentence to life imprisonment. The Governor has notified this board that he has reviewed your case. We have received his response." The Officer paused for a moment, but to Chester, it seemed like an hour. "Chester, we regret to inform you that the Governor did not accept our recommendation. Therefore your sentence of death by hanging shall stand. The date for your execution will follow shortly." The Officer then removed his glasses and sadly looked a morose Chester squarely in the eyes. "I'm sorry Chester, but we tried. There is nothing more to be done."

With his spirit crushed, Chester slowly made his way back to his cell, wondering what it would feel like to die. He already had an image in his mind from the time he had seen his cousin hung. It seemed like an eternity between the moment that the horse galloped away leaving his cousin to dangle from the end of the rope, and when he finally stopped kicking and jerking. His aunt's screams seemed to echo for hours. He remembered his brother leading him away from the horrible scene as the horrified screams haunted him through the dark night. Chester hoped that his own death would be quick. For a fleeting moment, he thought he would beat the law to the punch and do it himself. He didn't want a crowd around to watch him die. He could imagine his mother, battling her way through the cheering white faces and running up to him afterwards. She would hold his broken neck in her arms and sob as she tried to avoid looking into his bulging eyes. The vomit spewing out of his mouth would stain her nicely starched dress. Then Hattie would join her and cry over his body. They would remember that his feet shook violently, and see the waste dripping from his body. Those would be their last images of him. Hattie would later have to tell their son that their daddy was hung for murder. Their son would then carry that image with him for the rest of his life.

"No," he thought. I will save them from seeing me die and living with those thoughts."

But in the back of his mind, he knew that he could never do it. All of his life he had been taught that God would forgive anything except for the taking of one's own life. He felt that if he committed suicide, it would be the ultimate sin and he would burn in hell!

News of Governor Pleasant's decision spread quickly. The press tried in vain to get a statement from him but he eluded them at every turn. Then, on the Saturday night following his decision, he attended a function at the Cosmopolitan Hotel. The press cornered him and continuously badgered him for a statement. Although he was cordial and was willing to speak about many other issues, he behaved like the politician that he was and dodged any questions about the case against the Negroes. "I cannot comment on that case," he said. "The investigations are ongoing and it would be improper for me to comment!"

Each day, Chester wondered how many days he would have until they killed him. He got his answer less than ten days later, when, on December 8, 1917 he got the news from the prison officials. Governor Pleasant had signed the death warrants of Mark Peters and Chester Tyson! The hanging was scheduled for March 1, 1918. They had less than three months to live!

The community met the announcement with uproar and protests!

The backlash was powerful, unexpected and swift. Governor Pleasant was baffled at the volume of daily letters, petitions and newspaper articles calling for him to reverse his decision. With the new information that the press disseminated almost daily, people felt like they had been duped into believing that the negroes had instigated the crime while the real murderer could be out of jail in less than 15 years. They openly wondered if the Governor was "on the take" from the wealthy Waller family or his political interests. Instead of subsiding, the protests became louder and stronger.

Governor Pleasant's popularity began to suffer. His political future was in question. After several weeks of hoping that the furor would subside, he decided that he needed to take action to quell the dissent.

Most of the backlash called for equal justice between the convicted negroes and the whites. It wasn't so much that people felt that the negroes should live. Their call for "justice" demanded that Henry Waller should die. And if Henry didn't die, no one should die.

Governor Pleasant decided to see if further action against Henry Waller was possible. On Feb 4, 1918, he sent a letter to Harmon Drew, who was the current District Attorney of Webster Parish, asking if Johnny Long and Henry Waller could be tried on other indictments for other members of the Reeves family.

"Mr. Drew," Governor Pleasant inquired. "Henry Waller has only been formally tried for murdering two members of the Reeves family, even though they have other indictments pending. Can't we try him on some of the other indictments? If the State proceeds with another trial," Governor Pleasant wrote, "it would be possible to get a capital punishment ruling against Mr. Waller."

While waiting for an answer from Harmon Drew, Judge William C. Barnett, who was now special council of the Caddo district, learned that there might be a glitch in the Governor's proposal to retry Waller. He quickly picked up the telephone and placed a call to Governor Pleasant's office.

"Governor, this is Will Barnett" he stated. "I'm calling to speak with you about potential plans to act on some of the other indictments against Henry Waller."

"Yes, Mr. Barnett! That is certainly under consideration" Governor Pleasant replied.

There was an audible sigh of frustration from Judge Barnett on the other end of the phone.

"Governor, I recall an agreement from the defense that Waller would not appeal his life sentence, and the DA would not act on any of the other indictments *unless* there was a new material development of facts against Henry Waller in this case." he said. "As it stands now, the defense can certainly show that all of the facts now known were known at the time of his trial. He would argue that just because the prosecution failed to present them does not mean that they are new facts!" he stated emphatically.

"But there must be some error within those proceedings that would allow us to act on at least one of the indictments!" Governor Pleasant insisted. "I've got my constituents on my back and a public that is outraged! Certainly something can be done!"

But Judge Barnett was adamant.

"You try that and you just might be disappointed." He cautioned. "Another jury might outright acquit and then what are you going to do? "

Governor Pleasant thanked Judge Barnett and placed the phone back on its cradle. Despite Barnett's objections, he felt that there had to be some way around the red tape.

However, one thing was certain. The date of the March 1ˢᵗ execution of Chester Tyson and Mark Peters was quickly approaching, and it would be impossible to retry Henry Waller or Johnny Long prior to that date. If the State needed the Negroes to testify at Waller's trial, the Governor would have to postpone the execution date.

On February 22, 1918, the newspapers shouted the headlines:

"GOVERNOR PLEASANT SIGNS STAY OF EXECUTION!"

The Governor set the new date for the execution to May 3, 1918, at high noon. He was confident that they could get a death sentence for Henry Waller and Johnny Long by that date.

Chester and Mark breathed a collective sigh of relief. They had received a reprieve! Their families remained hopeful that this was the first step to a release. Mariah took the stay of execution as a sign that God had listened to her prayers and that He wouldn't let them kill her son.

However, when May 1, 1918, two days before their new execution date arrived, there had been no news of a trial set for Henry Waller. And there was no news from the governor of another reprieve!

Chester prepared for the execution. His countdown began and he suffered silent anxiety attacks as visions of his death swirled around in his head. He didn't want to die. Every moment, he imagined how the noose would tighten around his neck. At times, it was too much. "I just want them to kill me and get it over with!" he thought.

Chester was set to die at high noon on May 3. As the 48-hour window drew near, Chester was given the privilege of not working in the fields on his "last two days". He was allowed to spend the day however he saw fit within the confines of his cell. His Chaplain would arrive soon and would help Chester commit his soul to the Lord.

Contrary to popular belief, he was given no choice for his "last meal". He spent a sleepless night in his cell, anxiously waiting for 8:00 in the morning to come so he could begin his preparations for his journey to the Noose. He had seen the platform before. The large, wooden apparatus allowed for the hanging of one or more convicts at a time. More than once, he had seen a body dangling from it in the morning sun. Chills went down his spine and the hair on his arms stiffened at the mere thought of it. Alternating between fear and resignation, he began to try to decipher exactly how many minutes he had left.

"Dying has got to be better than living in this place!" he reasoned as his eyes watched a mouse crawl across the cell. "If I can just stand the pain for a few minutes I will soon be in a better place!"

A moment later though, he was not so brave. "What if it takes me an hour to die?" he feared. Chester met each moment with anguish. Each minute of the next few hours was filled with a different emotion.

The sun was shining brightly on the morning of May 3. Chester was wide awake as dawn broke through the dark night. At seven o'clock sharp, a guard brought his breakfast and slid it through meal slot in the metal bars. Chester barely glanced at the food, focused instead on a word, a glance or some indication from the guard about his fate. Receiving not so much as a sideways squint, he continued to pace in his tiny cell. The guard removed his uneaten breakfast about an hour later, again without as much as a "hello."

Knowing the noon hour was fast approaching, Chester alternated between huddling in prayer in the corner of his cell and pacing the floor. He nervously waited for the footsteps with the jangling keys that would take him to his death. Finally, at 11:00 am, the footsteps came. Chester's heart was in his throat as the keys turned in the heavy lock. Three guards stood next to his cell, ready to take his shaking body down the long hall, to face his execution.

"Lets move, Chester." one of the guards ordered. But Chester stood motionless.

"I said let's move, Chester!" the guard bellowed as he gave Chester a little push. Chester had heard the guard's first request, but his feet seemed to be glued to the ground. The push that the guard gave him was a much needed one, because he could not have begun that walk on his own.

He followed the guard out of the cell as the two other guards stood aside, and then followed Chester from the rear. Wordlessly they lead him down a long hall, and into a small room, bare except for a small table in the center, and several chairs on either side. A telephone, a notepad and a pencil graced the otherwise bare table. Mark was sitting in one of the other chairs. Chester assumed that this was where they would brief them and they would receive their instructions on how they planned to kill them.

One of the guards placed a welcome chair under Chester's wobbling body and then sat silently behind the desk. Chester and Mark sat on the same side of the room, in close proximity, but did not dare speak to each other. About 5 minutes later, the ringing telephone broke the silence in the room. The guard answered the phone and glanced at Chester.

"Yes Sir, they are." he flatly stated to the person on the other line, as he glanced at Chester and Mark.

"Yes, I understand." He continued. "We will see to it at once." He hung up the phone, keeping his eyes fixed on Chester.

"Chester and Mark," he said, his voice seeming to grip Chester's beating heart.

"That was the Governor Pleasant on the phone. Both of you have been granted a stay of execution until further notice. You will be returned to your cell at this time."

It was all Chester could do to keep from crying from joy, relief, and pure stress. He glanced out of the side of his eyes to try to get a glimpse at Mark, but Mark was staring straight ahead, apparently dealing with his own emotions.

On the way back to his cell, Chester thought about how close he had come to dying. His first reprieve, for the March 1st hanging had been received well in advance of the execution date. Never had he actually thought he was on his way to his death. But this time, he had no such advance.

"Maybe Mama prayed it away!" he thought as he walked back to his cell.

Mariah *had* prayed. She prayed hard every day of her life. A few days ago, Mariah and Mark's mother, Harriet, had called on others in their church and their community to pray with them. The following day, their "prayer circle" began. Everyone in her church, and many of her neighbors took up the charge of taking turns, praying in ten-minute slots. Every slot was filled, with many periods having two or three people, each praying during their given time. Charged with this most important task, they stopped wherever they were and went down on bended knee. It was not unusual to see someone in the fields cast down their hoe and fold their hands in prayer.

Mariah remained in prayer through the noon hour of May 3, scheduled execution time, even as the hour came and went. When she arose from her knees, little did she know that her prayers had already been answered. It would be another several hours until she learned that her son was still alive.

On May 9, 1918, Governor Pleasant signed the order for the execution for Chester and Mark. The new date was August 9, 1918.

Three months! Chester had ninety more days to ponder his certain death. "Surely," he thought, "I have seen the last of the reprieves." After facing death twice, he had become somewhat cynical to the process. Staring death right in the face on May 3rd had changed him. He just wanted it over! He didn't want to live any more. Each day was torture. What kind of life was it, that day in and day out would have man rise up in the morning and sweat in the hot sun until the sun went down? Was it really worth it to lie on the cold hard bunk, and relinquish half of his 6 x 8 cell to the rats, and critters that came out regularly? In the darkness of the cellblock, the days were as dark and gloomy as the nights, and depression and disparity was the order of the day. On Sunday, he had the privilege of solitary confinement for all but one hour of the day. During that hour, he had little contact with others, and when he did, it was of no consequence. Was it worth it to never be with a woman again, or hear the laughter of a child? He felt like he was in slavery. He didn't belong to himself. He belonged to the system. And like the ancestors who had been enslaved before him, he longed to be free.

The days clicked off, one by one, each exactly like the one before it. When August 8, 1918 rolled around, Chester reflected on his previous two scheduled hangings. He had walked away from both of them, each time worse for the wear. Tomorrow was hanging day. But this time seemed different somehow. Sadly, Chester realized he just wanted it done. If he was going to hang, just do it already! He was ready to die. Most prisoners in Angola died before their prison term was up because of the harsh prison conditions. No, he would rather die now. One more day and his misery would end.

Chester rationalized that everyone would be better off with him dead. Mama would have some closure. She would rejoice that he was with the Lord and she would thank God for it. Hattie would be free to move on without feeling guilty. Perhaps she would find a good man to take care of her and have a large happy family.

His life was a waste, now. He thought about Mama's insistence when he was younger, that he go to school twice a week instead of working in the fields. It was a one-room schoolhouse, with children of different ages taught in separate areas. He loved his teacher, Professor Powell. Professor Powell worked very hard at teaching the Negro children their lessons and was well respected by all. Chester had loved school. But what good had it done him?

His thoughts turned to the first time he met Hattie. He thought she was pretty but she didn't like him much. But that didn't last long. Hattie was only fifteen when she first got pregnant. Their baby, a boy contracted pneumonia and died at an early age.

With a start, he heard the guards coming down the hallway. Their keys jingled loudly on their belt loops as they strolled towards his cell announcing their approach.

They stopped on either side of his cell and sat in the chairs that had been placed there. They pulled out a writing tablet, and poised their pencils above it.

"Yeah, I'm still kicking!" Chester joked.

"Ok, let's keep it that way for now!" they joked back.

"Death Watch" was a peculiar phenomenon in prison. It usually began a few days before a scheduled execution. Several days before the date, the prisoner was usually pulled off work duty, if they were not already in solitaire. The last days would be spent in your cell unless you were lucky enough to have visitors. You were supposed to be able to request a choice for your "last meal." Though limited to a few selections, it was said to be ten times better than the usual grub.

The day before the execution, guards were stationed around you continuously to make sure that you did not commit suicide before they had a chance to kill you. Chester found some humor in that policy. You were going to die anyway, so what did it matter?

That was the phase that Chester was in now. They were here to make sure he didn't kill himself.

"No worries about me doing it!" Chester thought. "I'm sure that they will do a thorough enough job of breaking my neck.

That night, Chester vacillated between fear and resignation. He lay on his cot and thought about his life over the past years.

Chester began his "death walk" the following day. Clad in the black garb that they had provided, he strode from his cell, passing a few of his cellmates.

"Hey Ches!" called out the prisoner next to his cell. "We got 7-1 odds that says you're a dead man this time."

"Yeah, and I'm gonna come back haunt yo' black ass tonight." Chester joked back as he continued his trek down the concrete floor.

It grew silent as Chester made his way closer to the holding area. Now familiar with the procedures, he fixed his eyes on the phone that sat silently on the desk. Mark was there and seemed to be taking the process in stride.

When the phone rang Chester and Marked both shot straight up. This was the moment of truth!

A moment later, Chester and Mark were headed back to their cells. Another reprieve! The Governor had decided not to kill them until Dec 13, 1918.

"Humm! Christmas in Heaven!" Chester thought about his next hanging date. "Might be nice!"

As Chester passed the "gambler" he paused.

"Looks like a whole lotta folks is gonna have to pay up!" he laughed. "That is, unless I'm a ghost! Boo!"

"Locked back into his cell, Chester pondered his next "death". It would be nearing the Christmas holidays and the town would be gaily decorated with bright lights and colorful ornaments. Parties would be held to celebrate the season. Mama would decorate the house, but her heart wouldn't be in it because her heart would be heavy with thoughts of her son's impending death.

But once again, it was not to be. On December 6th, 1918, Governor Pleasant changed the date of the scheduled December 13th execution, resetting it to May 30, 1919. Then a few days before the May 30 hanging, Chester was reprieved until August 9, 1919.

"They kill me every August!" Chester quipped on his way back to his cell after hearing of the latest reprieve.

He and Mark took it all in stride. They had become jaded from the process and took each day as it came. They had gotten as far as the platform twice, before the Governor called off the execution off at the last minute.

Seven days before their August 9, 1919 hanging, two guards retrieved them from their cells, explaining that they were scheduled for a court appearance in the Webster Parish Courthouse. They were to ready themselves to be transported by automobile for the hearing. This bit of news was baffling. Why were they going to Minden? Both Henry Waller and Johnny Long had long completed their trials. They weren't witnesses in any other trials that they knew of. As far as they knew, their business in Minden was done.

As they pulled into the Minden courthouse, memories of their past filled their heads. Memories were fresh of that fateful night of Christmas Eve, 1916. That was the night that had changed their lives. As they exited the automobile, they both looked around for any signs of familiar faces, but they did not see anyone that they recognized. Finally, they entered the courtroom, and noticed a few unfamiliar faces sitting on the stiff benches, and staring at them as they walked to the tables in front of the little swinging doors. They had become familiar with a few members of the press and also noticed them sitting in the courtroom. Their pens were perched in front of them, no doubt commenting on how horrible Chester and Mark looked after being locked up for almost three years. Soon the bailiff entered from the side door and faced the spectators.

"All rise!" he commanded. Judge Sandlin entered and took the bench and then everyone reclaimed his or her seats.

The judge rattled off the case number for the stenographer and then began his briefing.

"We are here in the presence of the accused to modify the judgement in the cases of the State of Louisiana vs. Chester Tyson and Mark Peters." he began. He turned his attention to Chester and Mark.

"Your conviction for the murder of the Reeves family on December 24, 1916, still stands, as does the sentence of death by hanging." he stated. However, at the time of your sentencing, the law fixed the place of the execution as Louisiana State Prison in Angola. The Louisiana State Legislature has amended the law in that respect. The law now requires that in the case of capital punishment, the execution must take place in the same Parish as the crime committed." He paused and glanced down at the papers in front of him.

"The date of August 9, 1919 for your executions still stands. However, the *place* of your execution is hereby amended. The execution will no longer take place at the Louisiana State Penitentiary in Angola. It will now take place here, in Webster Parish at a venue set by the Sheriff. You will be remanded to the Webster Parish jail until said time of your executions. It is so ordered!" The judged banged his gavel and exited the courtroom without as much as a backward glance.

Chester and Mark exchanged glances.

"What the hell?" Chester questioned.

"I—I-- What just happened?" Mark was as confused as Chester.

Seven days! In just seven days, they would stand before their friends and family as they hung by the neck! Suddenly, it was more than just dying. They would be executed in their own back yard! Their closest kin would come and watch. Their families had usually steered clear of the prison, but now, they would feel compelled to come and witness the last breaths of their loved ones. Neither time, nor distance would prevent their appearance. With all of the reprieves that Chester and Mark had received, most people in the community just waited until an official word was released about their status. Five times they had been told that the hangings had been called off. But unlike the Louisiana State Penitentiary in Angola, Minden was right in their community. This time they would want to see it for themselves.

Each step that got them closer to the August 9th execution was excruciating. The black "hanging suits" seemed blacker. The sunny days seemed gloomy. During the 24-hour death watch, Chester once again found himself trying to figure out how he could end his own life in his cell before he had to stand before his executioners. He finally understood why the 24-hour watch was necessary. It was one thing to hang and die in private with a few strangers present. It was quite another to climb up on a scaffold and be hung in front of your friends and family looking on.

Chester's minister, Elder Harris visited him that evening. It was very different from his previous visits by the prison chaplain. Chester dreaded this visit. He did not want to look at the man of God who had known him since he was a child. He was afraid of the disappointment that he would see in his eyes. Chester vowed that he would do his best to explain why he had no choice in accompanying Henry Waller to the Reeves home that night. Hell! Everybody knew that Henry was crazy enough to kill Chester if he refused to go. Chester would again deny having anything to do with the murders, but he knew that doubt would linger in Reverend Harris' mind.

Once Reverend Harris arrived, Chester was grateful that the visit focused on his relationship with God, and not his involvement in the crime.

"Blessed are the pure at heart for they shall see God," the minister reminded Chester as he quoted Matthew 5:8. "Chester, your heart is pure and you shall enter the Kingdom of Heaven." he promised. "Let not your heart be troubled."

Chester did feel better after the visit. He knew that Mama was a woman of faith. Elder Harris would comfort her after his death. He felt a sense of calmness as he thought about one of Mama's favorite sayings: "This too shall pass."

Breakfast arrived at what seemed like an ungodly hour of the morning. The smell of the scrambled eggs and fresh biscuits made Chester want to puke. He imagined throwing up as the noose tightened around his broken neck. The thought of it was too much to bear. His plate was untouched when the guard collected it an hour later.

From his jail cell, Chester could see the crowd begin to gather below. Several of John Reeves brothers were there, no doubt to cheer as Chester and Mark suffered unbearable pain. Several children ran about the courtyard, playing tag or skipping rope as if it was just an ordinary day. In the distance, Chester noticed three people walking slowly down the road. Their stride looked familiar. Two tall colored men flanked a colored woman on both sides. With a start, Chester realized that it was Mama! Tears began to roll down his face as he witnessed Mariah's unsteady gait as she made her way towards the courtyard. She took slow steps, as if she were walking to her own execution. Frank and Bud seemed to be doing their best to ensure that her knees would not buckle beneath her. This was too much to bear! "Why would Frank and Bud allow her to come?" Chester angrily wondered.

The guards stationed outside of his door were engaged in light conversation just to pass the time of day. Their banter abruptly stopped when Sheriff Phillips and Sheriff Hughes arrived to take Chester to the noose that would end his life.

Mark was already in the hallway. Slowly they began their descent down the back stairs and walked behind the heavy curtains that had been placed about to hide them from view. Every step felt heavy and their hearts thumped wildly in their chests. Finally, they climbed up the steps and onto the platform. Chester avoided looking out into the crowd and instead fixed his gaze upon the black hood that the guard held in his hands. Elder Harris began to pray aloud.

"Yea, though I walk through the valley of the shadow of death, I will fear no evil; for thou are with me. Thy rod and thy staff, they comfort Me." the minister prayed. He continued to pray softly as the two executioners approached.

"Chester, Mark, do either of you have any last words before your death?" the first executioner asked.

Chester thoughts began to swirl around in his head. Should he apologize to the Reeves' brothers for the death of their family? But how could he do that without it sounding as if he was responsible for something that he didn't do? Should he just focus on his mother and assure her that he had committed his soul to heaven? He glanced over at Mark. Mark was staring straight ahead.

Silently, Chester shook his head as the executioners lifted the black hoods in unison and placed them over the heads of Chester and Mark. His heart began to thump, as the excited buzz in the crowd grew louder and louder. Under the darkness of the hood, Chester tried to determine what was going on around him. He listened for the footsteps indicating that the executioner was walking over to the lever that would release the bottom from the guillotine. He figured that when he heard the sound of the lever creaking, his feet would drop and he would suddenly feel the noose tightening around his neck as his feet dangled in the air.

He hoped it would be quick. While the thoughts continued to swirl around in Chester's head, he suddenly felt a warm burst of air moving across his face, and saw the bright sun shining brightly directly into his eyes. Startled, he realized that his hood had been removed, and he found himself once again looking out over the crowd. His executioner was rushing to the end of the platform, still clutching Chester's hood in his hand. After reaching the end, he bent down his head and nodded as he intently listened to the Sheriff. Seconds later, he began frantically motioning towards the executioner who was standing next to Mark. He was waving his hands across each other from side to side, apparently signaling him to stop the proceedings and wait for further instructions. Seconds later, the second executioner removed Mark's hood.

Chester looked out at the spectators. Their attention was focused on the commotion that was taking place on the side of the platform. Chester's mother, Mariah was looking up towards the heavens obviously in prayer while tears streamed down her face. A chain reaction of whispers was moving from one official to another. Finally, Chester's executioner walked back over to the center of the podium and faced the spectators. Sheriff Phillips and a few of the deputies joined him on the platform.

"Ladies and Gentlemen, may I have your attention please?" Phillips called out, his voice shaking and his eyes wide.

"It has just come to my attention that the Governor of Louisiana has issued a stay in the executions of Mark Peters and Chester Tyson." At this time, the prisoners will be returned to lock-up at the Webster Parish jail until transportation can be arranged to return them to the Louisiana State Prison. That's all folks! There is nothing more here to see. I will take a few questions from the press.

"Sheriff Phillips!" one of the reporters shouted. "Does this mean that the governor has decided against execution and has commuted the sentence to life?" was the first question.

"No, Sir, it most certainly does not." the Sheriff said. "The governor has indicated that a new date for the executions will be announced shortly."

All eyes were fixated on Sheriff Phillips as he took additional questions from the press. The crowd was barely aware of the four deputies who had retrieved the prisoners from their killing block. Reporters continued to barrage the sheriff with questions about the status of the hangings.

With wobbly knees, Chester and Mark were escorted from the platform, and lead away from the scene. They were badly shaken. They had come closer than ever to meeting their maker with their mothers looking on. Chester felt a knot in the pit of his stomach.

When Mark and Chester arrived back at the Webster Parish jail, the deputies took them to a meeting room and pointed each of them to opposite tables in the room. The deputies lifted their hands up on top of the tables and connected their wrists to the chains in the center.

"You have visitors," he announced.

"A few moments later, a deputy led Chester's mother Mariah, and Mark's mother Harriet into the room. They sat across from their sons, tears of relief streaming down their faces.

"You ok?" Mariah asked, concern for Chester evident in her cracking voice.

"I'm fine, Mama." Chester assured her. "Jest worried about you, that's all! Mama, why did you come!" he reprimanded her. "I didn't want you to see me like that. You weren't supposed to come!" he repeated.

"Son, I jest felt like I had to come and pray. A mother's prayers can change things. Besides, I would have never accepted it unless I saw it. And I needed to hold you one last time in my arms. It would have been the only chance I would ever have again to do that."

"Mama I don't think you understand how horrible it is to see a man hang! You wouldn't be able to take it Mama!" Chester reiterated. "There is nothing worse than to see a man hanging by his neck."

"Don't you think I know dat, Chester?" Mariah shot back.

"Chester, I was jest a child in slave times when I seed dat. Seed it mo'en once. I seed men hung. I seed a pregnant woman hung. Seed little chillun hung! And there weren't no chances for a reprieve! They weren't no hoods to cover da eyes. Dere was jest a noose and a whip!" she cried.

"Yeah, Son, I done seen it! And I know you want to protect yo' Mama from the ugliness, but ugly has been a part of life from the day I was born, and it's gonna stay ugly even afta I'm gone. You can't shield me from ugly!" she stated. "I had to come!"

"How's Leonard, Mama?" Chester said changing the subject. "And the girls?"

"They's doin fine, Son." she said. Mariah grew silent, apparently trying to process her next words to Chester.

"But Chester, there is sumpthin' I need to tell you." she said softly. It's about yo grandmamma Mealy."

"Chester, I hate to tell you this, but yo granmama passed away on May 29. Twas the day befo' you's supposed to be hung da last time. We stayed up late that night with her. We knew 'twert be long. But she had an easy passing. She told me some things bout her life that I ain't neva know'd before. Yo' granmama was a strong, strong woman! She lived bout

189

sixty somethin years in slavery, and then ova forty years out of it! Best she could figure she was born in about 1804. We found that out when we looked at her old Bible, and remember what her ol Massa say. We done carved her gravestone. It's a nice stone. It say "Mealie Banks, 1804-1919."

"Lord, Have Mercy!" tears rolled down Chester's cheeks as he thought about his grandmother. It always seemed like she was immortal. She could pick more cotton then men half her age, and chop cane without breaking a sweat. She always said that today's kids were too soft. Chester loved to sit on her lap when he was a small boy and listen to the stories that she told him about the slave days. Most of the old folks shooed you away when you asked them about the slave days, but not Big Mama! She would tell you the unvarnished truth, no matter how horrible it was.

"Was it tuberculosis?" Chester asked, knowing that many had died from the disease in recent months.

"Naw. I jest think she was ready to go on home. She was tired. I think she had planned to lead you to heaven that next day 'cause she went to bed with a prayer on her lips for you. She passed away in her sleep. She's buried up at Newsome Cemetery right next to yo little baby."

Chester and Mariah talked about family for a bit longer. Then the deputy arrived and led her away.

Soon, Sheriff Phillips appeared with a manila folder clutched in his hand. He sat down in front to Chester and opened the folder.

"Chester, Governor Pleasant has reset your execution date for March 24th 1920. Deputies from the Louisiana State Penitentiary will bring you back here a few days before that for preparations.

Mark and Chester boarded the train back to Baton Rouge later that evening. When they arrived, they were surprised to learn that news of their near-death experience had preceded them.

"Damn! nigger, how many lives you got?" another prisoner called out.

"More than a cat!" Chester joked back.

The prison rumor mill was that Governor Pleasant had "run out the clock" on Chester's and Mark's executions for his term, choosing instead to "pass the torch" on the case to whoever the new incoming governor would be. There would be a sixth reprieve before March 24th, and Chester and Mark would face hanging number seven. The new Governor would take office in May 1920. Then he would inherit the case.

The election process for the new Governor was heating up. The contest was between John M. Parker, democrat and J. Stewart Thompson, the Republican. In the Democratic stronghold of the south, it wasn't much of a "contest". Parker whipped Thompson with more than 97% of the vote, and took office on May 11, 1920.

Parker's major focus was on Women's Suffrage. He opposed it. He felt that women were not knowledgeable enough in "men's politics" and it would be a disservice to the country to allow them access to the ballot.

Also of great importance was the rise of Ku Klux Klan. A strong presence in the State since emancipation in 1865, the Klan had become stronger and more of a problem. Because of the great amount of influence that they had, it was usually political suicide to oppose them. However, they had come under fire for the sheer volume of lynchings that had recently occurred. Lynchings were numerous and frequent. The Klan used lynching not only as a tool to punish perceived crimes, but also as a tool to intimidate blacks, and prevent blacks from obtaining or keeping land. They also used it as a tool to collect a real or imagined debt, or for retribution against so-called "uppity niggers" who refused to conform to the status quo.

Parker had decided to sponsor an anti-lynching bill and put a stop to many of the ways that the Klan conducted their business. He aimed to show that he was a different kind of Governor.

With this in mind, Parker turned his attention to the list of items left undone by the Governor Pleasant's previous administration. He had carefully followed Governor Pleasant's actions while Pleasant was in office and he was aware that the Tyson and Peter's cases were still pending. Governor Pleasant had failed to act, choosing instead to keep some of his political capital by avoiding the issue. Governor Parker had decided that he would be proactive. Pushing the red button on his telephone, he activated the intercom connected to his secretary.

"Miss Foster?" he called into the mouthpiece of the phone. "When Judge Sandlin arrives will you show him right in?" he requested.

"Certainly, Governor Parker." she answered.

Judge Sandlin arrived promptly for the meeting, resting his hat on the desk. He slid into the seat across from Governor Parker.

Governor Parker opened his folder.

"I have in front of me the Tyson Case." he began. "And it appears that this case has been open since 1916 and the accused have been reprieved, let's see…." He said looking down at his file. "Seven times?!" he was incredulous. "Seven times an execution was stopped?! Now I got a new execution date coming up in a few weeks. You care to weigh in on this, Sandlin?"

"John, I think you know my feelings about the matter." Judge Sandlin said, dropping the formalities and reverting to the first name basis befitting of their friendship.

"It's a matter of record that I pushed for commutation of the sentence. At the time of the Negro trial, Henry Waller and Johnny Long had not yet been tried. Neither the public nor the jury knew that Waller was the real ringleader of the crime. The jury had some idea, but was limited by my admonishments about inadmissible evidence. Hell, the bodies weren't even cold yet when the negroes were tried. I actually thought that they might hang 'em all. They chose to hang only two because they had doubts as to whether the other two were there at all."

Governor Parker looked back down at the papers on his desk. "But I see no evidence of a motion for appeal in this case." Governor Parker said. "Why was there no motion for appeal? At least for Larkin Stewart and Anderson Heard. Drew could have moved for a directed verdict. A review could have surely found a reversible error!"

"I'm sure that their attorney had his reasons for declining to do that." Judge Sandlin said, thinking about the political blow that J. Webster Stewart's legacy would have taken if he continued to defend four negroes accused of a white murder.

"I'm sure he did." Parker said, apparently thinking the same thing. "In any case, I still have a problem to solve. "Do I commute? Or Execute?"

"Well John, as I said before, absent retrying Waller and Long, which now looks like it won't happen, my opinion is that the most expedient thing to do would be to commute. You already have the recommendation from the pardon board and other prominent citizens to do just that. Frankly, it wouldn't cost you much, politically. Most people think that the Pardon Board's word is the final decision anyway. And you would be perceived as a decisive figure and a fair man, if you make a definitive decision." Sandlin paused to observe the Governor deep in thought.

"On the other hand," Sandlin continued, playing devil's advocate in the process. "There is the matter of your stance on the anti-lynching bill. Many people abhor that bill and feel that you should oppose it. They don't want the Federal Government interfering in the State's business. The members of the Klan are certainly opposed to it and they have a lot of influence in this state no matter what some people feel about their methods. You don't want to antagonize them any more than is necessary."

"Well, you've been a great help!" Governor Parker sneered sarcastically. "You've said much but helped little. What am I to do?"

"That, Sir, is why you are the Governor!" smiled Judge Sandlin. "It is your decision to make."

When Sandlin left, Governor Parker once more reviewed the file on his desk. There were various reports and detailed recommendations from the Pardon Board. There were angry letters from citizens venting at Governor Pleasant for stopping the executions. There were even more letters from both citizens and members of the legislature weighing in on the case and pushing for commutation. Governor Pleasant reached into his file cabinet and pulled out a form. He stared down at it for a moment and then swiftly moved his pen across the bottom of the page. He picked up the telephone and relayed the news.

Three days later there were new headlines about the case.

"Mama!" Frank called out entering the front door of Mariah's house." "Mama look!" he held a newspaper up for Mariah to get a glance at the front page.

"What is it son?" Mariah said wearily. "Another one of those articles talking about Mark's supposed 'death'? Mark's poor Mama was scared to death last month when that newspaper from Kentucky reported that he went crazy and committed suicide. She was hysterical and went running up there to that jail, and there was Mark, healthy as an ox and wondering what she was blubbering about. They'll do anything to sell a newspaper!"

Mariah stuck a hand in the oven to make sure it was hot enough for the biscuits and then slid them into the oven.

"No, Mama, this one's a local paper. And they's talking about it all over town. See for yourself Mama!" Frank insisted as he held the paper under her nose.

Mariah stared at the headlines in disbelief. She could not believe her eyes as she glanced at the words written in big bold letters on the front page of the newspaper that Frank held in his hands! But she wasn't quite sure of what to make of the words written across the page.

"NEGROES NOT TO DIE"

"What's this?" Mariah asked, afraid that she was reading too much hope into the caption. "They changed the date again?"

"No, Mama!" Frank said impatiently. "Governor Parker commuted the sentence. They ain't gonna die at all! They'll be out in a few more years!"

Mariah sat in stunned silence for a moment, attempting to make sense of this information. Suddenly she pumped her palms towards the sky with her head thrown back.

"Praise God!" Mariah exclaimed. "Thank you Lord!" she shouted towards the heavens as she snatched the paper out of Frank's hands and collapsed on the sofa. She moved her eyes over the first few lines. Satisfied that it indeed said, "commuted" she jumped back up and did her happy dance!

When she calmed down a bit, she glanced over to a jubilant Frank. "But what does this mean for they jail time?" she asked. "What you mean by "a few more years?"

"Mama, they already done four years!" Frank reminded her."

"A life sentence in this state is no more than twenty years. But the parole board don't have to hold to that. They can cut that in half with good time. Good time can cut it to ten years and six months." he explained. Mariah was still staring at him, waiting for the rest.

"Now, I figure that the parole board already showed em some favor by pushing for the Governor to commute. With good time, they can be out in six more years. They might even get off sooner if Governor Parker

Mariah finally let herself hope. She felt optimistic for the first time since Christmas day in 1916.

Chester's spirits were also lifted when the news was delivered to him in prison. The Warden had delivered it personally even before the board called Chester in for his official change in status.

The change meant that Chester could leave death row. The general prison population was very different from death row. He would have privileges. He could interact more with the other prisoners and eat meals with the others instead of getting them through a slot in his small cage. He would be allowed use of the yard for more than just an hour a day on Sunday. Most of all, he would never again have a hood over his head or a noose around his neck while his friends and family looked on. Yes! This was cause for celebration!

Chester felt that with "good time" he could be out in less than ten years. Hell! He could do ten years and still be young enough to enjoy the rest of his life.

As August of 1920 came around, Chester marveled that he wouldn't face the noose *this* August. *This* August he was counting off the days until his release!

CHAPTER 12

SURVIVAL

Chester thrived in the general prison population. That is, as much as a "lifer" can "thrive". Four years on death row had been hell, and he felt liberated to some degree. Within a few years, he attained the status of Prison Guard and he felt that he was on his way to an early release. Being a guard meant that he avoided many of the hot days working the farm. He had not been in any serious trouble. He was doing his time. He worked in the kitchen occasionally, which afforded him the opportunity to gain favor with the other prisoners by slipping them an extra desert every now and then. Chester didn't leave himself out of the deal either. He ate pretty well for a prisoner!

One day he was particularly happy with the fare. It was near Christmas in 1921 and the turkey looked moist and succulent. Chester had just reached the front of the line and decided to sneak himself an extra piece of turkey when the server's back was turned.

"Tyson! Step out of line!" The Warden bellowed. Sheepishly, Chester dropped the meat he was holding and stepped out of the line. The Warden sent him to the rear of the line and made sure that Chester was served dead last! That meant no meat for Chester. Damn he was hungry. Other than that, he didn't have too much trouble with the rules.

On the other hand, he learned that Johnny Long had *major* problems with the rules. Chester was once more working in the kitchen when on June 22, 1922 he heard that Johnny Long had escaped. Johnny had just vanished without leaving a trace.

"Good for him." Chester thought. "Kid probably did 20-odd years

197

in his five. He probably ended up some big guy's playmate.

Hattie came to visit him every now and then. However, the visits had become less frequent, and Chester suspected that she had found someone else to keep her warm at night. But Chester appreciated the visits because it always provided news from home. As happy as the family was about the governor commuting Chester's sentence, some dissenters in the community were still very unhappy with the outcome. They wanted the Tyson, Heard, Peters, and Stewart families gone from the Grove community! And they were determined to ensure that they made it as uncomfortable as possible for the families.

Mariah had long ago declined the neighbors "invitations" to "find them somewhere more comfortable to live." Mariah was determined to live on the land on which they had worked so hard. But their hard work literally went up in smoke on one warm summer night.

Mariah had just come in from putting some tools away in the barn. She sat down on the sofa to rub her aching feet. Bud and his wife Josie had moved in with her some time ago to watch out for her after Chester's arrest. They were sitting on the divan across from her. Suddenly what sounded like a hundred horses galloping along became closer. Mariah ran outside just in time to see the horses encircle her barn. Perched on top of the horses were men dressed in white robes and carrying torches. White hoods with burned out holes over the eyes covered their heads. It was the Klan! The men on the horses were whooping and hollering, and then suddenly one of them threw his torch against the barn.

"Mama! Get back here!" Bud shouted.

Mariah ran back into the house and Bud quickly shut the door behind her. He swung the two by four piece of wood across the door frame to barricade it and then pushed the sofa up against the door. He ran into the bedroom, grabbed his shotgun and peered out of the window to see if the men were coming towards the house. The flames on the barn rose higher and higher. Satisfied, the men finally rode off on their horses.

Seeing that they had left, Mariah, Bud and Josie grabbed buckets and dipped them into the well that sat next to the side of the barn. With the water, they attempted to douse the fire. The barn held all of their tools. Bales of cotton that they had harvested all season were sitting inside and ready to market. Pieces of furniture, Bibles, and artifacts that had belonged to Mariah's mother Mealy were neatly boxed and ready to be distributed to her grandchildren come Christmas time. All of it went up in smoke! The fire was too big and too hot to put out. The fire left nothing except horseshoes and ashes! Feeling defeated, they headed back into the house, shaken by the violence that had been heaped upon them. Alternating between fear and resolve, they talked through the night.

Mariah decided to stay and rebuild. They had done it once – they could do it again. They would get more tools and more wood. It would be a tough winter, but it wouldn't be the first time. They could pull together as a family and make due. They began the process of recouping their loss.

But Mariah and her family suddenly found that they were being denied the basic materials and necessities that they needed to rebuild. The white neighbors who usually bought wood from them for heat in the wintertime were not coming by as often or at all. They got their wood elsewhere. Neighbors seldom invited the boys in the family to pick up extra work by picking cotton or chopping cane. And when they did, there were often false allegations of theft against them. Some were even followed by arrest! The Farmers Bank and the local white residents denied them credit.

And it wasn't just about the money. The police frequently arrested the colored men in the neighborhood for many other crimes that they had not committed. Mariah suspected that some of the whites were attempting to criminalize her sons and lock them all up for good. Little did she realize that the scheme went much deeper than she thought.

Mariah opened her door one day to find detective Bazer on the other side of it. He handed her some papers, and said, "You've been served, Ma'am."

Perusing the summons Mariah learned that one of her white neighbors intended to foreclose on her property, claiming that Mariah owed him money for a loan on some tools and had never repaid him.

"I didn't take out no loan!" she protested. "Nobody ever gave me no loan. I own this property free and clear! I don't owe nothing to nobody!"

"According to this, you and your family borrowed money and have not paid it back." he said. "There are several liens on your property that must be paid right away or your property will be foreclosed." Detective Bazer said, turning on his heels and walking away.

Confused, she called out to Bud.

"Bud, do you know anything about a loan we supposedly took out against the property?"

"No Ma'am! You know I borrowed tools and things from the Lewis' and the McGee's to get the work done around here. And we live off of what we grow! You know those white folks ain't gave us nothing on credit!" he stated.

"Well I just got this summons. It says that we owe them $667 dollars for tools and supplies. It says if we don't pay the money to the court in ten days that they have the right to foreclose on this farm. Oh, my God Bud. The same thing happened to the Harris'! They are trying to take our land!"

"They cain't do that Mama." Bud insisted. We have a legal patent for this land, and we don't owe no money to nobody. They can't just take our farm!" he repeated.

"They can, and they will!" Mariah said sadly. "The Harris' owned over 300 acres. They fought the white folks in court and lost. The court appointed the very man who was suing them to be personal representative over their estate and the man signed the property over to hisself and got away with it! The Judge rubber-stamped it and they lost most their land. It is just a matter of time before they lose the rest. If they can take it from the Harris', they can take it from us!"

Mariah threw the papers on the table and went back into the kitchen. She pulled the flour and salt out of the pantry and measured it into a bowl. She poured water from the little tin cup into it, and began to knead the bread.

"What are you doing, Mama?" Bud asked staring at her as if she had lost her mind. "We got to figure this thing out!"

"I'm making bread. Ain't nothing to figure out excepin' where we gonna go. Now hand me that lard over there."

Before his eyes, Bud saw the fight go out of his mother's eyes. It wasn't like her to give up without a fight. This was not a good sign. It was up to him to rectify the situation.

Ten days later, they had their day in court. Bud and Frank, flanked Mariah on either side as she stood up and told the Judge that she had not borrowed any money against the property or otherwise. She protested the fact that the court had appointed one of the white men to whom she supposedly money, as Personal Representative over her property.

"Your Honor," she pleaded, "The Personal Representative has a personal stake in this case. We would like to choose our own Personal Representative."

"Denied." the Judge stated flatly. "Judgment is for the plaintiff in the amount of $667 plus court costs and attorney's fees. If Judgment is not paid in full by close of business today, said property is hereby transferred to the plaintiff. It is so ordered!" he banged his gavel on the block, signaling that the case was closed.

Mariah left in tears and headed home to give her family the news. Many of them decided to move across the State line to Arkansas, much like Frank had done all those years ago. They had visited Taylor, Arkansas many times and found it to be much kinder for Colored people than Minden was. Sure, Taylor had its problems but the chances to be strung up on a rope were much smaller.

They put up a few trailers on one of the few lots of land in Grove that was still in the family. Then, a few families at a time found homes in Taylor and left Grove.

On December 26th of the following year, Bud arrived at Angola Prison to visit his brother, Chester. Bud usually came to visit around Christmas time, and brought Chester a little something from home. Chester was happy to see him even though he hated Christmas time since the murders. Bud's demeanor was different this year. He was usually chipper and talkative when he visited, but this year he looked drawn and was very quiet.

"Things ain't too good at home, Chester." he began. "We done lost the farm. White folks took it. Took ours and Aunt Georgia's too! I done moved most of the family across the line to Taylor. Me and Josie done found some land there and I think we's gonna be able to make it work. It ain't like Louisiana, Chester. Colored folks can have a little something in Arkansas.

"I can't believe you got Mama to leave that place!" Chester proclaimed. "Mama loved that farm!" She said that she would be there til the day she died."

Bud hung his head, and looked like he was deep in thought.

"Chester, see that's the thing. I come here today because I had to tell you something." Bud paused, and took a deep breath. "Chester, I hate to tell you this, but Mama passed away night before last. She never could bring herself to leave Grove and after we lost the farm she moved in with Georgia in a trailer. She'd been sick off and on for the past year or so. I think everything that she was going through was too much for her to bear. She just couldn't take it anymore, Chester. I'm sure she died from a broken heart. But her family was all around her when she passed."

Chester fell silent for a long time. Tears filled eyes as he realized he would never see his mother again. He looked up and took in his surroundings. Angola was a dreary place. The concrete walls were cold and uninviting. The "art" on the walls consisted of handwritten admonitions that warned the prisoners and visitors of every action that was mandatory or disallowed at the prison. The room smelled of stale cigarettes and yesterday's sweat. Several prisoners had visitors, some with children milling about. The children seemed oblivious to the nature of their surroundings. But the adults were aware. Some chatted incessantly, and some sat in uncomfortable silence. Finally, Chester looked over at Bud and spoke. "I'm sure Mama is in a much better place, now." he said sadly. "We should be happy for her that she is gone from this place, and is with the Lord."

They talked a little more about what was happening at home, and then Bud left. He went back to his farm in Taylor, and Chester went back to doing his time at the Prison Farm. He wondered what would be left to go home to after his time was done. His grandmother was dead. Mama was dead. Hattie had likely found someone else. The home he had grown up in and had known all of his life was gone.

Still, Chester continued to count off the days. He tried to keep up with the changes in technology and life outside of the prison walls, but mostly it was "prison as usual".

In December of 1926, Chester learned that Henry Waller had died in Prison of tuberculosis at the age of 43. No one came to claim his body and he was buried at the Angola Prison cemetery.

'He's dead. Good! I hope he rots in hell!" Chester lamented. He reflected on his own ten years in prison. Both of the white men who were responsible for his fate had escaped from their hellhole after serving less than 10 years. Johnny had escaped, probably with the help of friends or guards, and Henry Waller had been "liberated" by death. And here, Anderson, Larkin, Chester and Mark still sat, somewhere between life and death. It was another reminder to Chester of a cruel world.

Pushing the thoughts out of his head, Chester concentrated on letting go of the bitterness and just "toughing it out." He continued to mark off each day on the calendar, looking forward to the ones that provided relief from the harsh treatment and the mundane routine.

The Angola Prison Farm had changed very little over the years. However, Mother Nature tried her best to change that fact early in the morning on February 28, 1927.

It had been a rainy February. On the 21st of that month, Chester reflected on the fact that almost exactly nine years ago he was preparing to make his way to the noose for his first hanging. His execution, that had been scheduled for March 1st had just been cancelled. He remembered how panicked and emotional he was at the prospect of hanging.

Now, ten years after the murders in Grove, there was a certain serenity about him. Some people would call it a "hardness" but Chester preferred to call it a "calmness". He had made peace with the past and had settled his soul into relative tranquility. He did his work and bidded his time. He always had to watch his back, and assert his authority, but he had attained a certain level of respect. He wore his "guard" image well.

There had been many changes in politics since Chester first arrived. Governor Pleasant had finished his term in 1920 and was replaced by John M. Parker. Governor Parker left office in 1924 and was succeeded by Henry Luse Fuqua. Fuqua died in 1926 and was replaced by Oramel Hinckley Simpson, who served until 1928.

Chester had come to realize that none of the political changes had improved his plight. He had long stopped following Louisiana politics in hopes of being released. Each new Governor focused a bit of attention on Angola Prison, vowing to change its reputation as the "bloodiest prison in America" but none of them had much success. Someone always wanted to study the Farm and "improve" it. The inmates were like pawns in a game. When "company" came, the Warden either threatened them with loss of privileges or beatings or enticed them with extra privileges, depending on his mood. Chester was just part of the machinery. The constant rigors of death row had fundamentally changed him. There is something about solitary confinement and having no one to talk to but God and oneself that was enlightening. When he reached the general prison population after cheating death seven times, he embraced it. He felt little. He feared nothing.

Now, Chester relished the rain outside because it matched his mood that day.

The rain began to fall harder and Chester could feel the darkness surround him in the already gloomy prison.

The following day the weather cleared. However, the weather bureau reported that that a fifty-mile levee front along the Mississippi River near Baton Rouge had been battered by choppy waves. This meant trouble for Angola because the 18,000-acre prison was surrounded on three sides by the Mississippi River. A threat of a breach in the levee was very real, and there wasn't much time to prepare for the anticipated rising waters and possible breach of the prison protection.

Every man needed to be prepared to help build up the existing levee which would be insufficient to withstand the possible thirty-foot crest.

Chester sprang into action! As a lifer, he had already been through several devastating floods at the prison, the most dangerous being the flood of 1922. He knew that the clear weather could be deceiving. Despite a lot of doubt and push back by some of the other prison guards, he managed to convince them that although the weather might look calm now, the danger was in fact real and rapidly approaching. At his urging and under his direction, they worked rapidly and efficiently. They shored up the areas with the materials on hand and managed to stave off most of the floodwaters that began to rise the next day. Then the unimaginable happened. The levee broke! Chester had prepared for that possibility and managed to use miscellaneous materials to shore it up and hold it in place. Because of their work, the damage to the prison was much less than had been expected, and the threat was over.

With great pride, Chester accepted his accolades for the work he had done on the flood. He beamed as he observed the words "Commanded High Water Fight" that the Warden had written in big bold letters on his records.

He would earn double good time for going beyond the call of duty. Chester hoped that the prison board would take notice of his work, and show him favor when his next parole hearing arrived. He had served more than the required ten years and six months.

When his hearing arrived, he made himself comfortable in the seat that the board member offered him.

"Have a seat, Chester." the board member absent-mindedly said to an already seated Chester. It was a familiar routine. The Parole Officers glanced up at him a time or two while they read over the entries in his chart.

"Let's see here," he looked down at the papers. "High Water Fight decoration 1922. Promoted to Prison Guard in 1924. Worked as Fireman in 1926. Commanded High Water Fight, 1927. Those are good accomplishments, Chester. Now let's look at the other side."

The other officer looked down at his notes. "Let's see," he said. "We've got stealing meat in 1921. I see you were reprimanded and sent to the back of the line. Must've been a hungry day for you, huh Chester." the guard laughed. "We also have a fight with another prisoner, and an incidence of insolence to an officer."

It was the third officer's turn to speak.

"Chester, you were convicted of the murder of Maude Reeves in 1916 and sentenced to capital punishment. Governor Parker commuted your sentence to life in prison in 1920. What that means is that you must serve up to 20 years, but you are allowed a certain amount of good time off your sentence. So, although you are within your rights to request parole, we must also view the seriousness of the crime. In view of your crime and the limited amount of time you have served, this Board has declined your request for parole at this time."

Chester was disappointed, but he took the denial in stride. He would try again in a few years.

He was hopeful when he learned that Anderson Heard was paroled on August 21, 1927, but at the same time, he knew that Anderson should have been released long ago.

When his next parole hearing came around in 1931, once again he had no expectations. When the board again denied his parole, he casually walked out of the hearing room and went back to work.

When April 18, 1936 arrived, Chester allowed himself to hope. In eight short months it would be twenty years since the murders and almost twenty years since his conviction. He had not received any other reprimands while in prison. He had earned more good time. This parole hearing might turn out differently, he reasoned.

It seemed like an eternity that the Parole Officers shuffled through papers before they addressed Chester.

Finally, one of them looked up at him.

"Chester, we have had the pleasure of your company for the better part of twenty years. The mission of Angola Prison is to rehabilitate prisoners to insure that when they are released, they lead productive lives. You have performed well during most of your time here." the officer said, looking down at his papers.

"Chester, the world has changed a lot in the last twenty years. Most men your age served in World War I." the second officer began. "Colored men have found a place for themselves in society and the good Negroes have done well. We think that you will do well, too Chester. Keep your nose clean and stay out of trouble. Congratulations boy, you are being released today!"

Although he had been waiting for those words, Chester could hardly believe his ears.

"Released?"

He could just walk out of that prison and not look back? It was too good to be true. But it was true. Moments later, he was walking off of the prison grounds.

CHAPER 13

THE LONG, LONG ROAD

The aroma of springtime met him at the prison gate. As he walked along the dirt road, he noticed bright flowers peeking out of the ground around him. Funny, he hadn't noticed how colorful springtime was in over twenty years. The sun was brighter. The morning air felt lighter.

He didn't know where he was going. He just wanted to walk. Instinctively, he headed north, towards Minden. He was headed home!

Chester had $2 in his pocket, and not a clue about what things cost, after being incarcerated for twenty years. He kept walking down the road until he reached a country store and sat down on the wooden bench outside. He watched people come and go and listened to their conversations unnoticed.

It was a good way to learn what was going on in the world. Many people were talking about the Scottsboro Boys, who had been imprisoned not far from Angola Prison. They had been accused of raping several white women. The consensus from white folks seemed to be that they should have all been lynched. The consensus from colored folks was that the all-white jury that convicted them was corrupt and that they were framed. For Chester, it seemed that not much had changed in twenty years.

Franklin D. Roosevelt's presidency seemed to have gained favor with the colored people. His "New Deal" was attractive to many of them. Chester heard people saying that Roosevelt had appointed positions to a great number of Negroes, but Chester doubted the truth of what he had heard.

209

Chester was surprised to hear that women had won the right to vote in 1929. Apparently, there had been contentious debates that resulted in a change to the constitution. Chester also learned that Indians had gained citizenship in 1924. Chester listened intently to the groups who talked about culture and politics as they came and went.

After listening to some of the talk around town, Chester headed towards the train tracks. A freight train was headed north and creeping slowly along the tracks. Chester hopped onto one of the cars when no one was looking and scurried towards the rear. Soon, the train picked up a bit of speed and Chester moved to the open door to get a look outside. He watched the trees go by, and soon he began to recognize the terrain. About an hour later, the scenery became very familiar as they neared the city of Minden. Chester hopped unnoticed out of the train as it slowed to a crawl. He strolled into the city, marveling at the new cobblestone roads. The number of automobiles whizzing by was a bit unsettling to Chester who was used to horses and wagons that had been the typical mode of transportation in 1916 Minden. Now, the automobiles jockeyed for space with the horses and buggies, creating a mishmash of transportation hazzards.

With a start, he passed the jailhouse and shivered as he remembered his near-hanging there years ago. Instinctively, he looked over to the courtyard to see if the noose still swung from the platform. Thankfully, it did not.

Chester headed for the old road that led the seven miles from Minden to Grove. As he walked along, he noticed the run-down houses and the neglected fields. The farms that once thrived with cotton and cane were now overrun with tumbleweeds and falling barns. White children were playing outside of many of the homes that had previously been owned by Chester's family and friends.

He passed several cemeteries along the way, and stopped at the one marked "Newsome Cemetery". Stopping to kneel at his mother's grave, he pondered how hard her life must have been near the end. She had lost her son to a bloody prison, and lost her land to corrupt white folks. He rose from his knees noticing numerous relatives in the surrounding plots, who had died while he was in prison.

Moving slowly along, he walked towards the old homestead. About fifteen minutes later he found himself in front of the old Reeves home. There it stood, empty, but otherwise appearing as it always had. To a stranger, it would have looked like any ordinary country cabin. To Chester, it looked like a house of horrors. He remembered the awful screams, and Miss Maudie running in terror from that house as Henry Waller chased her down like the devil himself.

Beginning to tire from his long journey, Chester noticed that the train had pulled up to the Grove whistle-stop station. He made his way to one of the cars. He would rest for a while and decide his next move. He curled up in the corner, exhausted from his day. Soon, he was fast asleep.

Chester awoke with a start, confused at first to see daylight instead of darkness and iron bars.

Alarmed, he felt the train jerk, signaling its departure. He quickly scurried towards the door, planning to jump out before the train picked up speed. When he looked out of the door of the car, he was greeted by a view of what was once Anderson's house. It was burned to the ground! A newer, nice brick house stood next to it, with white children running about in the fields. Then, moments later, the train reached his old homestead. The yard was overgrown with weeds. The fields were neglected and brown stalks stood amidst yellowing leaves in the field. Gone was the beautiful fruit orchard. The barn had been reduced to ashes from the wrath of the Klan. Near the ashes, his own house, once neatly trimmed and filled with love and laughter, had collapsed on one side and sat empty and dilapidated. There were no children running about. With a start, he realized that his and Hattie's child would be grown now. Hattie was probably happily married! Saddened and confused, Chester slid back into the corner of the freight car and rested his back against the bags of grain that were stacked there.

He stared straight ahead and did not move a muscle as the train picked up speed. He stayed where he was when the train slowed down again about an hour later. He refused to look outside again until he was further away. Much later, as the train continued on its way, slowly bouncing over the tracks, Chester finally looked out of the car. But he looked ahead. He refused to look back.

He would ride until he felt that the time was right to get off. He didn't know how long he would ride. He didn't care how far he would go. But Chester knew one thing for sure. Wherever he was going had to be a million times better than where he had been!

Afterword

Few descendants of Mariah Tyson's family remain in Grove, Louisiana today. Many of them moved to Taylor, or other parts of Arkansas. Some moved to Houston, Colorado, or California. The effects of the murders, still linger within the family today, as the Legacy of Chester Tyson is told to the children and grandchildren.

Chesters Tyson and Mark were both released on from Angola Prison on April 18, 1936. Each had served nearly 20 years, which was the maximum they could have served for their "Life" sentence at that time.

Anderson Heard served nearly 10 years.

Henry Waller died of Tuberculosis in Louisiana State Prison on December 2, 1926, after serving about ten years. He is buried in the Prison Cemetery.

Cody Reeves drowned on July 25, 1920, in the Dorcheat Bayou River. His death came less than three years after the murder of his family.

Johnny Long escaped on June 22, 1922, without leaving a trace. He had served less than five years.

The family never regained their property. In fact, many of the descendants of the family never knew that there were over 600 acres of land that ended up in the hands of others largely due to the unequal justice that was the order of the day during those years. Many relatives died landless and broke, and today, are buried in pauper's graves and nearby cemeteries.

The good news is that I did complete my mission to find out more about my grandmother. I located Grandma Kitty's (Mariah's) grave, as well as her mother, Mealy's grave. Although the belief was that Grandma Mealy lived to be 115 years old, I have found slave records that put her age closer to 108, which still, was a lifetime both in and out of slavery.

My research continues. There is still much to be written in hopes that my descendants will know their history. When I wrote *Ten Generations of Bondage: Eleven Generations of Faith,* I chose one central ancestor to focus on in each generation. My goal is to eventually expand upon the lives of those ancestors who endured extraordinary heartache. Chester Tyson's story was greatly expanded beyond the few paragraphs that it received in *Ten Generations.* I hope that within this book, I have answered many of the questions that will continue to be asked by his descendants.

Johari Ade

People vs Chester Tyson

www.ingramcontent.com/pod-product-compliance
Lightning Source LLC
Chambersburg PA
CBHW030009290326
41934CB00005B/274